FOOD
FOR
SHOW

food on the go!

FOR THE BENEFIT OF
MOUNT SINAI AUXILIARY'S ONGOING
COMMITMENT TO THE DEVELOPMENT OF
METROPOLITAN-MOUNT SINAI MEDICAL CENTER

MINNEAPOLIS, MINNESOTA

Third Printing

Published by
Mount Sinai Auxiliary
2215 Park Avenue
Minneapolis, Minnesota 55404

612/871-3700

Printed by Bolger Publications/Creative Printing
Minneapolis, Minnesota 55414

Betsy Breckenridge Norum, recipe consultant
Andrea Tranvik Bolger, calligraphy
Barbara Ellerin, logo design

Library of Congress 83-060257

ISBN 0-9610854-0-1

FOOD FOR SHOW!
food on the go!

"Food for Show/Food on the Go" is a cookbook reflecting the needs of today's creative and involved society.

The cookbook was conceived by the Mount Sinai Auxiliary to tap the culinary talents of its diverse membership and to provide a long term fundraiser to help meet the auxiliary's commitment to the Development Fund.

Participation from an enthusiastic community has provided the committee with delicious old and new recipes that have been tested, tasted and chosen to fit into today's busy lifestyles. This unique cookbook lets you treat family and friends to delectable foods often thought too difficult to try — even on busy days filled with work and activities. Recipes in each section have special notations of whether it's for "show" or "on the go" to indicate the committee's definition of ease in preparing each recipe.

Special thanks go to the many volunteers who have shared their knowledge, talents and ideas to organize, test recipes, type, edit and proofread the cookbok. It is truly a collaboration that represents the vitality, creativity and commitment of the Mount Sinai Auxiliary. It's a cookbook to "show" the Auxiliary "on the go!"

To order additional cookbook copies, use order blanks in back of the book or write to:

> Cookbook
> Mount Sinai Auxiliary
> 2215 Park Avenue
> Minneapolis, Minnesota 55404

The price of each book is $9.95 plus $1.25 postage and handling. (Minnesota residents please add 60¢ sales tax per book.) Checks should be made payable to: Mount Sinai Auxiliary.

Organizations and retail stores wishing to purchase the cookbook, please write to the above address.

Mount Sinai — a name that since the time of Moses has symbolized a gift and a responsibility.

In that tradition Mount Sinai Hospital was founded in 1951 as a gift from the Jewish people to the people of Minnesota. With its dedication, the hospital assumed its continuing responsibility and commitment to excellence in healing, teaching and research.

In January of 1988, Mount Sinai Hospital merged with Metropolitan Medical Center to form Metropolitan-Mount Sinai Medical Center. Hand in hand with the new hospital family, the Auxiliary continues to be a visible support in implementing its goals of service to the patient, the hospital and the community. These goals include health education, public relations, fund raising, and volunteer services. With over 2,000 members, the Auxiliary is the largest hospital auxiliary in the Twin Cities.

The future holds promise of new growth and development. Metropolitan-Mount Sinai Medical Center and the Auxiliary will continue to make a significant contribution in providing new programs and services and responding to the ever changing needs of health care.

Mount Sinai

AUXILIARY

COOKBOOK COMMITTEE

CHAIRPERSON
Marcia Cherniack

TESTING CHAIRPERSON
Sandy Goodman

COORDINATORS
Fremajane Wolfson
Judy Harris

MARKETING CHAIRPERSONS
Muriel Wexler

FOREWORD AND HISTORY
Arlis Grossman

TREASURER
Frances Finkelstein

EDITOR
Sue Zelickson

ASSISTANT EDITORS
Sheila Paisner
Delores Sigel

CONTRIBUTORS, TESTERS, THOSE WHO HELPED

Ruth Aaron
Meryll Abelson
Myrna Abrams
Ruth Abry
Florence Alch
Lynne Alpert
Ida Altrowitz
Marian Altrowitz
Bonnie Axelson

Kerry Bader
Scott Bader
Arlene Badiner
Shirley A. Baker
Ardis Barnett
Linda Barrows
Joan Baskin
Patti Baskin
Joanne Bauman
Mabel Bauman
Edith Beirstein
Linda Benenson
Cathi Benson
Leona Berle
Charlotte Berman
David Berman, M.D.
Shirley Besikof
Joan Binder
Sura-Fraida Blatt
Arline Bloom
Percy Bloom
Andrea Bolger
Lou Ann Bongard
Linda Braufman
Carroll Britton
Ann Bronstien
Sylvia Bronstien
Cindy Brown
Ricki Butwinick

Susan Calof
Esther Capp
Ruth Cardozo
Edith Carlson
Harriet Cherniack
Marlys Cohen

Rusty Cohen
Verene Cohn
Jeanne Corwin
Sheila Corwin
Joan L. Cotroneo

Harriet Davis
Jodi Davis
Haddie Derechin
Laurie Derechin
Marnie Desnick
Mitzi Diamond
Susan Diamond

Ceil Edwards
Wendy Engel
Marja Engler
Jan Ephraim

Cindy Fegley
Francine Feinberg
Frankie Filister
Harvey Filister
Irene Finberg
Marion Fisher
Linda Fiterman
Susan Fiterman
Sunny Floum
Pat Foulkes
Barbara Frank
Nancy Friedell
Margie Frishberg

Chicky Galinski
Pam Gallop
Hazel Garner
Minette Gaviser
Peni Gensler
Cindy Ginsberg
Barbara Gleekel
Lois Goldberg
Rivian Goldberg
Rivoli Golden
Diane Goldenberg
Eva Goldenberg
Judy Goldenberg
Cindi Goldfine

Cookie Goldman
Susan Goldman
Florence Goldstein
Renie Goldstein
Toni Goldstein
Annette Goodman
Beatrice Goodman
Lois Goodman
Shirley Goodman
Baylee Gordon
Jane Gordon
Margie Graceman
Etheldoris Grais
Babette Gross
Susan Grossman
Sylvia Grossman

Arlene Harris
Charlotte Harris
DeeDee Harris
Jane Harris
Jean Harris
Joye Harris
Natalie Harris
Sue Harris
M. Olivine Hayes
Linda Hechter
Pearl Heitke
Bea Herman
Valerie Herschman
Elliot Herstein
Min Himmelman
Jackie Hirsch
Ruth Hirsch
Arlene Hockenberg
Doris Hodroff
Diane Hoffman
Lori Holliday
Ethel Horne
Helen Horwitz
Linda Hyatt

Diane Ingber

Eva Jacob
Jane Jacobs

Joan Jaffee
Ellen K. Joseph

Ruth Kaiser
Diane Kaplan
Helene Kaplan
Joy Kaplan
Lil Kaplan
Rose Kaplan
Sandy Kaplan
Vicki Kaplan
Raleigh Karatz
Stephanie Karon
Esther Kates
Anne Katz
Maxine Katz
Sherry Kehr
Delores Kelber
Marcella Killen
Roberta Kirschbaum
Doris Kirschner
Charlotte Klein
Marion Klein
Dianne Kline
Ruth Knelman
Donamae Koppelman
Peter Kordell
Devie Koval
Celia Krank
Myra Krank
Roberta Kravitz
Annetta Krelitz
Micki Kronick
Winnie Kuppe
Judy Kuretsky
Marcee Kutner

Joan LaBelle
Natalie LaBelle
Elaine Landy
Edith Latts
Janet Leavitt
Mimi Lebewitz
Miriam Leff
Roxanne Leopold
Ruth Levinson

Many thanks!

Perri Levitus
Sharon Levitt
Dorothy Levy
Kay Levy
Lucky Levy
Marcia Levy
Sheila Lieberman
Miriam Link
Erma Lipschultz
Joni Lipschultz
Sybil Lipschultz
Sue London
Petrena Lowthian
Sandy Lurie
Carolyn Luther

Gail Machov
Renee Maisel
Joyce Malmon
Phyllis Mandel
Daisy Marcus
Helen Marhley
Marilyn Marker
Nancy Markowitz
Marjorie Marles
Ruth Mayeron
Leslie Melamed
Hiram Mendow
Josephine Mendow
Ardene Meshbesher
Naomi Meyerson
Ann Miller
Paulette Mitchel
Marlene Moscoe
Joyce Moscoe

Candy Nadler
Edith Nadler
Sooky Narvey
Nancy Nathanson
Annette Neff
Suzanne Nemer
Harriet Newman
Joan Noun

Barry Paisner

Charleen Paisner
Hy Paisner, M.D.
Martin Paisner, M.D.
Joyce Peck
Mary Lou Peilen
Joyce Perlman
Enid Perlmutter
Ferne T. Pesses
Jane Peterson
Bea Pink
Dorothy Pink
Lisa Pinsky
Jane Pistner
Marion Pollack
Marie A. Pudil

Gayle Rapoport
Susan G. Rappaport
Cheryl Ravich
Rollie Rinkey
Terry Rivard
Maryen C. Rivkin
Clara Roberts
Dona Rodich
Janice Rodkin
Sybil Robinson
Barbara Rosenberg
Phyllis Rosenblatt
Linda Ross
Tudie Ross
Gale Rothman
Pam Rothstein
Marilyn Rovner
Barbara Rubin
Elaine Rubin
Jana Rubin

Nancy Saliterman
Bertha Salsberg
Sylvia Samuels
Connie Sandler
Patti Sandler
Joanne Savitt
Bea Schimmel
Jack Schneck, M.D.

Marian Schneck
Eileen Schribman
Tina Schwartz
Lorraine Schweitzer
Carol Segal
Gloria Segal
Louise Segal
Lynne Segal
Robin Segal
Shelley Segal
Joyce Segalbaum
Marcia Shainock
Bernice Shapiro
Bonni Shapiro
Judy Shapiro
Rona Sher
Doris Sherman
Nancy Shiller
Darlene Schwartz
Lil Sigesmund
Shirley Silberman
Sara N. Silverstein
Marlen Simon
Susan Simon
Minnie Singer
Jessica Sipkins
Hazel Skarman
Maxine Smiley
Ethel Smith
Rollee Smith
Lynn Snyder
Sharon Snyder
Alicia Spitzberg
Ellyn Stein
Roz Steinfeldt
Elaine Steinman
Margie Stengold
Ione Stiegler
Jean Stillman
Liba Stillman
Marilyn Stillman
Ruth Stillman
Esther Straus
Cooky Strimling

Phyllis Sudit
Bruce Swanson
Dorothy Swatez
Annette Sweet
Betty L. Sweet

Marsha Tankenoff
Mollie Tankenoff
Paula Tankenoff
John C. Tidemann
Jean-Claude Tindiller
Joanne G. Topp
Mulvien Trach
Toodie Trestman
Karen Triebar
Rollie Troup
Margaret Tucker

Nancy Unterman

Peggy Vermes

Abby Walden
Lil Warschauer
Jackie Wartnick
Wanda Weick
Judie Weil
Margie Weil
Gail Weinberg
Judy Weiner
Joan Weinstein
Sue Weinstein
Phyllis Weisberg
Margery Weisman
Charlotte Weiss
Elaine White
Connie Wilensky
Goldie Wolf
Elizabeth Wolfson

Marcia Yugend

Margie Zats
Barry Zelickson
Penny Ziessman
Bonnie Ziskin
Sylvia Zouber

"GRANDMA'S CURE"

Rheumatism, Sniffles, The Gout and Psychoses
Lumbago, Hypertension, Rhinitis, Neuroses
Globus Hystericus, Heartburn, The Croup
All boils down to Grandma's Cure . . .

Chicken Soup *see page 20*

Contents

Show ■ Showy for company

Go ■ Easy for busy days

Appetizers

TEX-MEX SPREAD

Show ■
Go □

2 (10½ oz.) cans bean dip, plain or jalapeño
1 c. dairy sour cream
½ c. mayonnaise
1 (1¼ oz.) pkg. taco seasoning mix
¼ tsp. garlic powder
3-4 ripe avocados
2 T. lemon or lime juice
½ tsp. salt
¼ tsp. pepper
8 oz. shredded sharp Cheddar cheese
1 c. thinly sliced green onions
3 med. tomatoes, seeded and chopped
2 (3½ oz.) cans chopped ripe olives

In shallow 9x13-inch serving dish, spread bean dip. In small bowl, combine sour cream, mayonnaise, seasoning mix and garlic powder; spread over bean dip. Mash avocados, add lemon juice, salt and pepper; spread over the sour cream mixture. Sprinkle with cheese, onions, tomatoes and olives. Serve cold or heated with tortilla or taco chips.

12 servings

Removing tomato seeds keeps spread from getting watery. A large quiche dish is perfect for this amount. For a very spicy dip, add 2 (3 oz.) cans chopped green chiles.

a real tastemaker

MEXICAN APPETIZER

Show ■
Go ■

1 (8 oz.) pkg. cream
  cheese, softened
1 (15 oz.) can chili without
  beans
1 (3 oz.) can chopped
  green chili peppers
½-1 bunch green onions,
  diced
1 (3½ oz.) can pitted ripe
  olives, sliced
½-1 lb. Monterey Jack,
  Cheddar or Mozzarella
  cheese, shredded
pitted ripe olive slices for
  garnish

Layer ingredients in order in 9-inch pie or quiche plate. Chill. Serve with crackers or taco chips.

8 servings

GUACAMOLE

Show ■
Go ■

3 ripe avocados, peeled
  and mashed
½ tsp. garlic powder or
  more to taste
1 T. medium salsa sauce
salt and pepper to taste
1 tsp. lemon juice
1 tomato, chopped

Combine avocados, garlic powder, salsa, salt, pepper and lemon juice. Place in serving bowl. Sprinkle tomato on top. Refrigerate. Serve with taco chips, pita bread or fresh vegetables.

1 pint

So easy to prepare!

SALSA

Show ☐
Go ■

2 med. tomatoes, diced
1 med. onion, diced
¼ c. chopped green
pepper
¼ c. chopped fresh parsley
1 clove garlic, crushed
½ tsp. salt
⅛ tsp. pepper
⅛ tsp. cumin powder
⅛ tsp. chili pepper to taste

Combine all ingredients in small bowl. Serve with tortilla chips.

3 cups

CHILE CON QUESO

Show ■
Go ■

1 lg. onion, chopped
2 cloves garlic, chopped
2 T. oil
salt and pepper to taste
2 (4 oz.) cans green chiles,
diced
1 (14 oz.) can whole peeled
tomatoes, drained and
chopped
1 (8 oz.) pkg. Monterey
Jack cheese
1 (8 oz.) pkg. Velveeta
cheese
1 (4 oz.) pkg. Longhorn
cheese

In 3-quart skillet, sauté onion and garlic in oil. Season with salt and pepper. Add chiles and sauté 2 minutes. Add tomatoes and simmer 10 minutes. Cut cheese into chunks and add to warm sauce. Cook on low heat until cheese is almost melted, but still is a little chunky.

Serve in a chafing dish with tortilla chips for dipping. For nachos, spread melted mixture on tortilla chips. Bake at 350 degrees for about 5 minutes or until bubbly.

1 quart

Some like it hot!

ROSEWOOD ROOM GRAVLAX AND DILL SAUCE

Show ■
Go □

1½-2 lb. fresh boned
   salmon side
¼ c. brown sugar
¼ c. salt
dash white pepper
1 tsp. ground celery seed
1 tsp. fennel seed
½ c. finely chopped fresh
   dill
1 c. oil

Dill sauce:
3 egg yolks
1 c. oil
¼ c. Dijon mustard
½ c. brown sugar
2 T. finely chopped fresh
   dill
Tabasco
salt
Worcestershire sauce

Place salmon in shallow pan, skin side down. Combine sugar, salt, pepper, celery seed and fennel seed; sprinkle over salmon. Cover with dill. Slowly pour oil over fish, cover tightly and refrigerate 7-12 days.

Make dill sauce by beating egg yolks until creamy. Slowly add oil, beating constantly to thicken. Add mustard, sugar and dill; season to taste with remaining ingredients. To serve, remove fish from pan and scrape away dill and spices. Pat dry. Cut salmon into thin diagonal slices with electric knife. Serve with dill sauce and black or rye bread.

10 to 12 servings

DILLED SHRIMP APPETIZER

Show ■
Go ■

1½ c. mayonnaise
⅓ c. lemon juice (or more
   to taste)
¼ c. sugar
½ c. dairy sour cream
1 lg. red onion, sliced
2 T. dill weed
¼ tsp. salt
2 T. capers
2 lbs. shrimp, cooked

Mix all ingredients, stirring in shrimp last. Refrigerate overnight. Serve with tooth-picks.

8-10 servings

May be prepared up to 48 hours in advance.

SPICY PICKLED SHRIMP

Show ■
Go ☐

1 lb. med. shrimp
2 lg. onions, chopped
3 cloves garlic, chopped
½ c. olive oil
½ c. cider vinegar
¼ c. white wine
5 fresh jalepeño peppers, sliced or 1 (4 oz.) can jalepeño peppers or green chiles
few dashes Tabasco (optional)
1 c. chopped green onions
lettuce
4-6 radishes, sliced
8-10 green olives

Clean and shell shrimp leaving tails on. In a large skillet over medium heat, sauté onions and garlic in oil for 3 minutes. Add shrimp and stir-fry until pink. Remove and place in medium size bowl. Add vinegar, wine, peppers, Tabasco and green onions. Cover tightly and refrigerate at least 24 hours, stirring occasionally. Serve on lettuce-lined platter garnished with radish slices and green olives.

6-8 servings

NANTUCKET CRAB MOLD

Show ■
Go ☐

1 (10¾ oz.) can tomato soup
1 envelope unflavored gelatin
¼ c. cold water
1 (8 oz.) pkg. cream cheese, softened
¾ c. mayonnaise
½ c. finely chopped onions
¾ c. chopped celery
2 dashes Tabasco
½ tsp. paprika
1 tsp. Worcestershire sauce
2 tsp. white horseradish
2 (6 oz.) pkgs. frozen snow crab, thawed

Bring soup to boil. Remove from heat. Soften gelatin in water. Add to soup; stir until gelatin is dissolved. Cool. Beat cream cheese until smooth. Add soup mixture and beat until combined. Add remaining ingredients. Pour into a greased 6-cup mold. Refrigerate overnight. Unmold and serve with crackers, party rye or pumpernickle bread.

10-12 servings

LE GRANDE TUNA BALL

Show ■
Go ■

1 (8 oz.) pkg. cream
  cheese, softened
1 T. chopped onion
dash Tabasco
¼ tsp. salt
1 (7 oz.) can tuna, well
  drained and flaked
¼ c. chopped ripe olives
¼ c. chopped parsley
1 c. shredded Cheddar
  cheese

Mix together cream cheese, onion, Tabasco and salt. Add tuna, olives and half of the parsley. Shape mixture into a ball. Combine remaining parsley and Cheddar cheese. Roll ball in parsley mixture and refrigerate for several hours or overnight. Serve with crackers.

8 servings

EGG SALAD MOLD

Show ■
Go □

12 hard-cooked eggs,
  chopped
1 c. Miracle Whip or
  mayonnaise
¼ c. minced onion
2 T. prepared mustard
1 tsp. salt
1 tsp. pepper
2 envelopes unflavored
  gelatin
½ c. cold water
½ c. plus 1 T. whipping
  cream, whipped
1 c. dairy sour cream
dash onion salt
12 olives
12 cherry tomatoes
Seafood Dressing (see
  index)

Combine eggs, Miracle Whip, onion, mustard, salt and pepper together and set aside. Sprinkle gelatin over water in small saucepan and heat slowly until dissolved. Cool slightly, mix with egg mixture and refrigerate. Fold whipped cream into egg mixture and spread into a greased 6½-cup ring mold. Refrigerate overnight.

Unmold on serving platter and frost with sour cream that has been seasoned with a dash of onion salt. Garnish with olives and cherry tomatoes. Serve with crackers or party rye. Place bowl of Seafood Dressing in center of mold.

10-12 servings

ARTICHOKE SQUARES

Show ■
Go ■

2 (6 oz.) jars marinated
　artichoke hearts
2 med. onions, chopped
1 clove garlic, crushed
4 eggs, beaten
½ c. bread crumbs
¼ tsp. salt
½ tsp. pepper
½ tsp. oregano
½ tsp. Tabasco
8 oz. shredded sharp
　Cheddar cheese
2 T. chopped parsley
grated Parmesan cheese
paprika

Drain marinade from one jar of artichokes into skillet. Discard remaining marinade. Chop artichokes and set aside. Sauté onions and garlic in marinade for 5 minutes. Combine eggs, crumbs, seasonings, Cheddar cheese, parsley and sautéed onions. Add artichokes. Pour into greased 8x8-inch pan. Bake at 325 degrees for 30 minutes or until set. Sprinkle with Parmesan cheese and paprika last 5 minutes of baking. Cut into squares and serve.

8-10 servings

HOT SPINACH SPHERES

Show ■
Go ☐

4 lg. eggs, beaten
2 (10 oz.) pkg. frozen
　chopped spinach,
　thawed and well drained
1 T. finely minced onion
¾ c. butter, melted
¾ c. grated Parmesan
　cheese
½ tsp. salt
¼ tsp. pepper
½ tsp. thyme
¼ tsp. nutmeg
dash Tabasco
2½ c. crumbled herb
　seasoned stuffing mix

Combine eggs, spinach, onion, butter, cheese, salt, pepper, thyme, nutmeg and Tabasco. When well blended, add stuffing mix. Stir and let stand 20 minutes or until slightly firm. Shape into walnut-size balls and place on ungreased baking sheet. Bake at 350 degrees for 20 minutes.

60 pieces

May be prepared ahead and frozen. Reheat at 350 degrees for 10-15 minutes.

COLD SPINACH MOUSSE

Show ■
Go ☐

2 T. oil
3 (10 oz.) pkgs. frozen
  chopped spinach
1 tsp. salt
½ tsp. pepper
½ tsp. nutmeg
1 sm. onion, grated
1 c. mayonnaise
1 T. lemon juice
2 envelopes unflavored
  gelatin
¼ c. water
1 c. whipping cream,
  whipped

Green Mayonnaise:
12 watercress leaves
6 sprigs parsley
13 spinach leaves
2 c. mayonnaise

Brush 6-cup ring mold with oil. Cook spinach according to package directions. Drain well; squeeze out moisture and chop finely. In large bowl, combine salt, pepper, nutmeg, onion, mayonnaise and lemon juice. In small saucepan, dissolve gelatin in water over low heat. Fold gelatin into whipped cream and combine with spinach mixture. Pour into mold and refrigerate 2 hours.

For green mayonnaise, drop watercress, parsley and spinach leaves into boiling water. Blanch 1 minute. Drain and rinse in cold water. Squeeze dry; chop and combine with mayonnaise. To serve mousse, unmold on serving platter and top with green mayonnaise.

6-8 servings

CHOPPED EGGPLANT

Show ■
Go ☐

1 med. eggplant
1 med. onion, chopped
2 cloves garlic
1 sm. green pepper,
  chopped
1 sm. tomato, chopped
1 tsp. salt
dash pepper
3 T. oil
1 T. vinegar

Prick eggplant and bake at 400 degrees for 30 minutes or until soft. Cool and peel. Chop eggplant in blender or food processor. Combine with remaining ingredients; cover and refrigerate at least 24 hours. Serve chilled with crackers or cocktail rye.

8-10 servings

EGGPLANT CAVIAR

Show ■
Go □

1 med. eggplant, unpeeled
   and diced
1 lg. onion, chopped
½ green pepper, chopped
2 cloves garlic, crushed
⅓ c. olive oil
1 tsp. salt
½ tsp. pepper
½ tsp. oregano
½ tsp. basil
1 T. sugar
1 (6 oz.) can tomato paste
¼ c. water
¼ c. vinegar
½ c. sliced stuffed green
   olives
1 (4 oz.) can mushrooms,
   drained and chopped
¼ c. capers (optional)

Combine eggplant, onion, green pepper, garlic and oil in large skillet. Cover and simmer for 10 minutes. Add remaining ingredients; cover and simmer until eggplant is cooked but not mushy, about 20 minutes. Chill and serve cold in lettuce-lined bowl as cocktail spread with favorite rye bread or crackers.

1 quart

CUCUMBER DIP

Show ■
Go ■

1 (8 oz.) pkg. cream
   cheese, softened
1 sm. unpeeled cucumber,
   chopped
¼ c. chopped green onions
salt
garlic salt

Mix all ingredients together by hand. Cover and refrigerate overnight. Serve with cut-up vegetables.

10-12 servings

ANCHOVY SPREAD

Show ■
Go ■

**1 (8 oz.) pkg. cream
   cheese, softened
2 (2 oz.) flat cans
   anchovies, chopped
1 tsp. lemon juice
dash Worcestershire sauce
1 generous T. Miracle Whip**

Blend all ingredients together by hand. Refrigerate for several hours. Remove 1 hour before serving. Serve with rye bread.

10-12 servings

CHICKEN LIVER PATE

Show ■
Go □

**2½ T. butter
5-6 shallots, peeled and
   finely chopped
1 bay leaf
1 lb. chicken livers
3 cloves garlic, chopped
½ c. cognac
2 c. whipping cream
3 T. finely chopped parsley
salt and pepper**

In a skillet over low heat, melt butter and cook shallots with bay leaf until soft. Do not brown. Turn heat to high and cook until translucent. Add chicken livers and garlic; sauté quickly on both sides.

In a small saucepan, heat cognac; pour over livers and ignite mixture with a match. Cook 1½ minutes, watching carefully. Douse flame by covering with lid. In a large saucepan heat cream; add to livers and bring to boil. Discard bay leaf. Add 2 tablespoons of parsley and salt and pepper to taste. Place ingredients in food processor and purée. Mixture will be soft. Spoon pâté into individual ramekins or 1-quart serving dish and refrigerate overnight. Before serving, garnish with remaining parsley. May be frozen.

1 quart

HERB CHEESE SPREAD

Show □
Go ■

1 (3 oz.) pkg. cream
   cheese, softened
¼ tsp. chervil
¼ tsp. chives
¼ tsp. chopped parsley
garlic powder, to taste

Blend ingredients together. Serve with crackers.

¾ cup

ANTIPASTO TO GO

Show ■
Go ■

1½ c. chopped ripe olives
1 c. chopped stuffed green
   olives
3 med. tomatoes, chopped
6 green onions, chopped
1 med. green pepper,
   chopped
2 T. tarragon vinegar
1 T. oil
Tabasco to taste

Combine all ingredients and place in bowl. Refrigerate for 24-48 hours. Drain off some of the liquid before serving.

1 quart

HERRING ANTIPASTO

Show ■
Go ■

1 (16 oz.) jar herring in
   wine sauce
1 med. green pepper,
   chopped
1 med. red onion, chopped
1 (2¼ oz.) can sliced ripe
   olives
1 (6 oz.) jar marinated
   artichokes, drained
1 (12 oz.) jar Bennetts chili
   sauce

Drain and cut herring into small pieces. Place in bowl and add green pepper, onion, olives and artichokes. Add chili sauce. Cover and refrigerate 2 hours or overnight. Serve plain or with crackers or cocktail breads.

4 cups

FANCY ANTIPASTO

Show ■
Go □

1 c. ketchup
1 c. chili sauce
1 c. water
½ c. olive oil
½ c. tarragon vinegar
½ c. lemon juice
1 clove garlic, crushed
2 T. brown sugar
1 T. Worcestershire sauce
1 T. prepared horseradish
salt to taste
dash cayenne
½ head cauliflower, cut
   into flowerets
3-5 carrots, sliced
   diagonally into 1½-inch
   pieces
2-4 ribs celery, sliced
   diagonally into 1½-inch
   pieces
1 (6 oz.) jar artichoke
   hearts, drained, cut into
   halves
½ lb. whole fresh
   mushrooms
1 (8 oz.) jar pepperocini,
   drained
1 (2 oz.) jar stuffed olives,
   drained
2 (7 oz.) cans tuna, drained

In large saucepan combine ketchup, chili sauce, water, oil, vinegar and lemon juice. Season with garlic, brown sugar, Worcestershire, horseradish, salt and cayenne. Bring to a boil and simmer a few minutes. Add the vegetables and simmer 20 minutes or until vegetables are tender. Add tuna and simmer a few minutes longer. Cool. Cover and refrigerate. Serve with crackers.

3 quarts

Will keep two weeks in refrigerator.

A little taste of Italy

13

PARTY HERRING SALAD

Show ■
Go ■

1 (16 oz.) jar pickled
   herring fillets, drained
2 apples, peeled and
   chopped
2 navel oranges, peeled
   and chopped
1 sm. red onion, chopped
8 oz. dairy sour cream

Cut herring into small pieces and place in a bowl. Add apples, oranges, onion and sour cream; mix well. Cover and refrigerate until thoroughly chilled. Serve with rye bread or crackers.

16 servings

CHUTNEY-CURRY CHEESE SPREAD

Show ■
Go ■

2 (8 oz.) pkgs. cream
   cheese
1 c. shredded sharp
   Cheddar cheese
½-1 tsp. curry powder
2 T. sherry
1 (9 oz.) bottle mango
   chutney
5 green onions, finely
   chopped

In double boiler, heat cream cheese, Cheddar cheese, curry powder and sherry until cheese melts. Spread on large round plate. Cover and chill. Before serving, spread chutney over mixture and sprinkle with green onions. Serve with crackers. May be prepared day ahead.

12-14 servings

WITH A BRICK OF CREAM CHEESE

Show ■
Go ■

1 (sm. or lg.) brick cream
   cheese
soy sauce and sesame
   seeds
         or
caviar and chopped green
   onions and sieved egg
   yolks
         or
Spiced Green Pepper Jelly
   (see index)

Place brick of cheese on a serving dish that has sides. Cover with topping of soy sauce sprinkled with sesame seeds OR caviar sprinkled with green onions and egg yolks OR Spiced Green Pepper Jelly; serve with your favorite crackers or rye toast.

4-8 servings

CHEESE STICKS

Show ■
Go □

¾ c. plus 2 T. butter
2 c. flour
½ tsp. salt
1 c. shredded Swiss cheese
3 T. grated Parmesan
  cheese
3 T. shredded Cheddar
  cheese
1 egg, beaten
2½ T. milk
1 egg, beaten
poppy seeds

In food processor or mixer, blend butter, flour and salt until crumbly. Add cheeses, 1 egg and milk, being careful not to over blend. Refrigerate dough about 30 minutes. Cut in half and roll out each part into an 8x12-inch rectangle about ¼ inch thick. Using a sharp knife or pastry wheel, cut into 3x½-inch strips. Place on foil-lined ungreased cookie sheets. Brush with beaten egg and sprinkle with poppy seeds. Bake at 375 degrees for 12 minutes or until golden brown.

7-8 dozen

May be frozen baked or unbaked. Do not thaw before baking.

BAKED GOUDA

Show ■
Go ■

1 (8 oz.) pkg. refrigerated
  crescent style dinner
  rolls
1 (7 oz.) Gouda cheese
1 egg white, beaten
sesame seeds

Using finger, smooth out perforated marks on dough to form solid rectangle. Remove casing from Gouda and place cheese in center of dough. Bring up all corners of dough to totally encase cheese, making sure all openings are sealed. Brush top with egg white and sprinkle with sesame seeds. Place on ungreased cookie sheet. Bake at 375 degrees for 30 minutes or until golden. Allow to sit a few minutes before cutting into wedges. For a variation, before closing the cheese, coat with several teaspoons of prepared mustard.

4-6 servings

HOT AND SAUCY SALAMI

Show ■
Go ■

**1 (2 lb.) Kosher salami or
  bologna**
½ c. tomato soup
½ c. vinegar
½ c. mustard
½ c. sugar
½ c. butter, melted
3 egg yolks, beaten

Remove casing from salami, score top and place in a shallow baking dish. In saucepan combine remaining ingredients and cook until thick, stirring constantly, about 20 minutes. Brush the sauce over salami. Bake uncovered at 350 degrees for 1 hour or until crusty, basting occasionally. Serve remaining sauce on the side.

12 servings

BAKED BOLOGNA OR SALAMI

Show ■
Go ■

**1 (1 lb.) Kosher bologna or
  salami, skin on**
½ c. apricot jam
¼ c. brandy

Cut bologna or salami in half lengthwise. Place in a shallow pan, rounded side up. Score top in several places. Mix together jam and brandy. Brush ½ mixture on bologna. Bake at 350 degrees for 1 hour, basting often with remaining mixture. Slice and serve. May cut bologna or salami in chunks; pour on mixture and bake.

4-6 servings

May add 2 tablespoons prepared mustard to jam and brandy mixture.

No baloney!

MEATBALLS SUPREME

Show ■
Go ☐

2 lbs. ground beef
½ c. water
1 egg
¼-½ envelope dry onion
  soup mix
½ c. bread crumbs
2 tsp. garlic powder (or to
  taste)
1 (16 oz.) can whole
  cranberry sauce
2 c. ketchup
½-1 c. water

In a large bowl, combine beef, water, egg, onion soup, bread crumbs and garlic powder. Shape into balls and place in a covered roasting pan. In a saucepan, combine cranberry sauce, ketchup and water. Bring to a boil and simmer 5 minutes. Pour over meat balls. Cover and bake at 350 degrees for 2 hours. Uncover and bake 1 more hour.

The meatballs freeze well. Bake 2 hours, cool and freeze. Defrost and reheat for 1 hour.

40 meatballs

WATERCRESS SANDWICHES

Show ■
Go ■

12 thin slices white bread
3 T. butter, softened
¼ c. chopped fresh
  watercress
1 (3 oz.) pkg. cream cheese
2 T. mayonnaise
¼ tsp. salt
¼ tsp. paprika
¼ tsp. curry powder
sprigs of fresh watercress
  or parsley

Remove crusts and flatten bread with rolling pin. Spread with butter. Combine remaining ingredients except sprigs in blender; spread on bread. Place small sprig of watercress on each end and roll up. Cut in half. Place on flat sheet and cover with damp towel. Refrigerate until ready to serve.

24 small sandwiches

CHINESE CHICKEN WINGS

Show ■
Go ■

1 c. water
1 c. soy sauce
1 c. brown or white sugar
¼ c. pineapple juice
¾ c. oil
1 tsp. ginger
1 tsp. garlic powder
20-24 chicken wings, cut in
    half

Mix all ingredients except chicken wings in a blender or food processor. Pour over chicken wings and marinate. When ready to bake wings, pour ½ cup of marinade on jelly roll pan, reserving the remaining marinade for basting the wings. Place the wings on top of the marinade. Bake at 350 degrees for 45-60 minutes. Brush with reserved marinade. These freeze very well.

12-15 servings

Finger lickin' good!

Soups
and
Salads

THAT SOUP

Show ■
Go ■

1 (3½-4 lb.) chicken, cut up
1 med. onion
2 carrots, sliced
1 parsnip, sliced
1 rib celery, sliced
1 T. salt
¼ tsp. white pepper
1 tsp. dill weed

Rinse chicken pieces well. Place in a 4-quart pot and cover with cold water. Bring to a boil and skim broth very well. Reduce to simmer and skim again. Add all remaining ingredients and cook until chicken is tender, 1-1½ hours. Remove chicken. Serve soup with the cooked vegetables and Matzo Balls.

3½ quarts

"EVERYONE CAN COOK" MATZO BALLS

Show ■
Go ■

2 rounded T. chicken fat
2 eggs, well beaten
2 tsp. chopped parsley
½ tsp. salt
pepper to taste
1 tsp. grated onion
⅔ tsp. baking powder
¾ c. matzo meal

Add chicken fat to eggs and mix in remaining ingredients. When well mixed, refrigerate for several hours. An hour before serving, shape loosely into small round balls and drop into rapidly boiling water for 15 minutes. Remove and add to hot soup.

20 matzo balls

"Everyone Can Cook" was the first Mt. Sinai Auxiliary Cookbook published in 1952

Say ah-h!

CREAMED TOMATO BISQUE

Show ■
Go ■

½ c. butter
1 c. chopped celery
1 c. chopped onions
½ c. chopped carrots
⅓ c. flour
2 (28 oz.) cans tomatoes,
   drained and chopped
2 tsp. sugar
1 tsp. basil
1 tsp. marjoram
1 bay leaf
4 c. chicken broth
2 c. whipping cream
½ tsp. paprika
¼-½ tsp. curry powder
¼ tsp. white pepper
salt to taste

Melt butter and sauté celery, onion and carrots. Add flour and cook 2 minutes, stirring constantly. Add tomatoes, sugar, basil, marjoram, bay leaf and broth. Cover and simmer 30 minutes. Discard bay leaf. Purée one half at a time in blender. Add cream, paprika, curry, pepper and salt. Serve hot or cold. Freezes well.

6-8 servings

May add shrimp or crab to bisque and heat through.

GAZPACHO

Show ■
Go ■

3 tomatoes, unpeeled and chopped
1 med. cucumber, unpeeled and chopped
1 med. onion, chopped
2 cloves garlic, crushed
1 (24 oz.) can tomato juice
⅓ c. wine vinegar
¼ c. olive oil
⅛ tsp. salt
¼ tsp. pepper
½ tsp. curry powder
1 c. mayonnaise

Blend tomatoes, cucumber, onion, garlic, 1 cup of tomato juice, vinegar and oil in food processor or blender. Add mixture to remaining tomato juice and season with salt and pepper. Chill overnight. Mix curry powder with mayonnaise. Serve Gazpacho in individual bowls topped with a dollop of curried mayonnaise.

8-10 servings

ZUCCHINI SOUP

Show ■
Go ☐

1 med. onion, chopped
¼ c. butter
4 c. chicken stock
12 c. shredded zucchini
½ c. chopped parsley
¼ c. dill weed
¼ c. basil
1½ c. light cream or half cream and half buttermilk
salt and pepper to taste

Sauté onion in butter until golden. Add stock, zucchini and seasonings. Simmer about 25 minutes or until tender. Let cool. Place in food processor or blender and purée. Add cream, salt and pepper. Chill at least 4 hours.

12-14 servings

For the diet conscious, use all buttermilk. May also be served hot.

ORIENTAL CELERY SOUP

Show ■
Go ■

**sliced greens and tops of 1
  celery stalk**
2 qts. chicken broth
2 c. diagonally cut celery
2 c. sliced fresh mushrooms
½ tsp. ginger
½ tsp. garlic powder
1 tsp. soy sauce
½ c. sliced green onions
½ c. torn spinach

Simmer celery greens and tops in broth for 30 minutes; remove from broth. Add sliced celery, mushrooms, ginger, garlic powder and soy sauce. Simmer 7-10 minutes until celery is slightly tender. Add onions and spinach and simmer 1-2 minutes. Serve immediately.

6-8 servings

May add water chestnuts, cut-up chicken or shrimp.

CUCUMBER SOUP

Show ■
Go ■

3 med. cucumbers, peeled
1 med. leek
2 T. butter
2 bay leaves
1 T. flour
3 c. chicken broth
1 tsp. salt
1 c. whipping cream
juice of ½ lemon
dill weed to taste
dairy sour cream

Slice two cucumbers and the leek and sauté in butter. Add bay leaves and cook slowly until mixture is tender but not brown. Stir in flour, broth and salt; simmer 5 minutes. Remove bay leaves, press mixture through a sieve and chill. Remove seeds from third cucumber. Shred and add to chilled soup. Add cream, lemon juice and dill. Serve with a dollop of sour cream.

4 servings

Soup's on!

WATERCRESS SOUP

Show ■
Go ☐

3 T. butter
¼ c. minced onion
3 bunches fresh watercress,
  washed and stemmed
1½ c. water
1 tsp. salt
½ tsp. white pepper
2 T. flour
2 (13 oz.) cans chicken
  broth
2 c. milk
2 egg yolks
1 c. whipping cream

In a large saucepan, melt 1 tablespoon butter and sauté onion until golden. Add watercress, water, salt and pepper. Cook over high heat for 5 minutes. Pour small amount of mixture into food processor or blender and chop. Do not purée. Remove from processor. Repeat chopping process for remaining watercress mixture.

In a large saucepan, melt remaining butter, stir in flour, add chicken broth and milk. Bring to a boil. Discard half of liquid from watercress mixture. Add remaining watercress mixture to broth. Beat egg yolks and cream together. Stir 1 cup of the hot soup into the egg-cream mixture and add it to the soup, stirring constantly. Heat thoroughly. Do not boil.

8 servings

BEEF LENTIL SOUP

Show ■
Go ■

2 lbs. stewing beef
3 T. flour
2 tsp. salt
¼ tsp. pepper
3 T. oil
5 c. water
2 c. sliced celery
5 med. carrots, sliced
2 lg. onions, chopped
1 c. lentils
1 T. lemon juice
1½ tsp. salt
1 tsp. thyme

Cut beef into ½-inch cubes. Dredge in mixture of flour, 2 teaspoons salt and pepper. Heat oil in large pot and brown meat. Add water, cover and simmer 45 minutes. Add celery, carrots, onions, lentils, lemon juice, salt and thyme. Simmer covered, 1½ hours or until meat is tender. Stir occasionally. More water may be added if soup is too thick.

8 servings

SALAMI SOUP

Show ■
Go ■

2 (13 oz.) cans Crosse &
   Blackwell minestrone
   soup
1 (10½ oz.) can beef broth
1 (15 oz.) can tomato sauce
   with bits
1 (15 oz.) can water
salt to taste
¼ tsp. pepper
¼ tsp. thyme
3 med. carrots, sliced
1 c. chopped celery
1 (8 oz.) can kidney beans
1-2 lb. salami, cubed
1 c. shredded red cabbage
grated Parmesan cheese

Place all ingredients except cabbage and cheese in large soup pot, cover and simmer for 2 hours on top of the stove or in the oven at 325 degrees. Five minutes before serving, add cabbage. Garnish with Parmesan cheese.

8 servings

May add 1 cup cooked pasta to soup.

SNIDER'S RESTAURANT, BEMIDJI
SHERRIED WILD RICE SOUP

Show ■
Go ■

⅔ c. wild rice
4½ c. chicken broth
1 T. minced onion
2 T. butter
¼ c. flour
5 c. chicken broth
¾ tsp. salt
1¼ c. cream
½ c. sherry
minced parsley or chives

Place wild rice in a strainer and rinse under tap water until water runs clear. In a large pot, bring broth to a boil, add rice and boil for 25-30 minutes. Stir occasionally. Drain and rinse in cold water. Set aside.

Sauté onion in butter until light brown. Blend in flour; add broth, stirring constantly, until thickened. Stir in wild rice and salt, simmer about 5 minutes. Blend in cream, sherry and simmer until heated. Garnish with parsley or chives.

8 servings

BEAN AND BARLEY SOUP

Show ■
Go ■

¾ c. dried lima beans
½ c. barley
2 qts. water
1 lb. soup meat
1 soup bone
4-5 dried mushrooms
   (optional)
1 med. onion, diced
1 med. carrot, diced
1 tsp. salt
pepper to taste

Thoroughly wash beans and barley. Bring water to boil in a 4-quart pot. Add meat, bone and beans. Boil a few minutes and skim. Add remaining ingredients, cover and simmer 2½ hours on top of stove or in oven at 325 degrees. Add salt and pepper. Cut the meat off the bone and discard the bone. Soup will be thick, add water to thin.

6-8 servings

BEER CHEESE SOUP

Show ■
Go ■

¼ c. butter
½ c. shredded carrots
¼ c. chopped onion
4 c. whole milk
½ c. flour
2 c. chicken stock
1 T. chicken bouillon
   granules
2 c. well-packed shredded
   sharp Cheddar cheese
1 tsp. Worcestershire sauce
2 dashes Tabasco sauce
salt and white pepper
1 (12 oz.) bottle strong
   beer or ale, room
   temperature
chopped green onions,
   Baco Bits and popcorn

Melt butter in a large saucepan. Add carrots and onion. Cook until onion is transparent but not brown. Transfer to blender or food processor. Add 3 cups of the milk and purée. Return to the pan. Add flour and blend well. Add remaining milk, chicken stock and bouillon. Cook over medium heat, stirring constantly, until it comes to a boil. Cook 2 minutes longer. Remove from heat, add cheese, Worcestershire sauce and Tabasco. Season with salt and pepper to taste. Just before serving, beat beer into soup with a wire whisk. Serve soup hot with side bowls of chopped green onion, Baco Bits and popcorn.

8-10 servings

COLD PLUM SOUP

Show ■
Go ■

1 (29 oz.) can purple
   plums, drained (reserving
   syrup), pitted and
   chopped
1 c. water
⅔ c. sugar
1 cinnamon stick
¼ tsp. white pepper
pinch of salt
½ c. whipping cream
½ c. dry red wine
1 T. cornstarch
2 T. lemon juice
1 tsp. grated lemon rind
1 c. dairy sour cream
3 T. brandy
dairy sour cream
cinnamon

In a saucepan, combine plums, reserved syrup, water, sugar, cinnamon stick, pepper and salt. Bring to a boil over moderately high heat. Reduce heat to moderate and cook mixture, stirring occasionally, for 5 minutes. Stir in cream. Mix wine with cornstarch and add to soup mixture, stirring until thickened. Stir in lemon juice and rind, remove pan from heat. In a small bowl whisk the sour cream and brandy into ½ cup of soup. Add the mixture to the soup and stir until smooth. Let the soup cool; chill it covered for at least 4 hours. Ladle into cups; garnish each serving with a dab of sour cream and a sprinkle of cinnamon.

6-8 servings

CURRIED CHICKEN SALAD

Show ■
Go □

2 c. diced, cooked
   chicken, dark meat
1 apple, peeled and diced
1 c. diced fresh pineapple
¼ c. golden raisins
⅓ c. chopped dates
2 T. chopped chutney
1 c. shredded coconut
½ tsp. salt
1 T. curry powder
2 T. chicken consommé
1 c. Mayonnaise (see index)
lettuce leaves

In a large bowl, combine chicken, apple, pineapple, raisins, dates, chutney, ½ cup coconut and salt. In small saucepan, mix curry powder and consommé. Simmer 2 minutes stirring into a smooth paste. Combine paste and Mayonnaise. Stir into the salad ingredients. Arrange lettuce leaves on serving plates and pile the salad on the leaves. Sprinkle with remaining ½ cup coconut.

4 servings

OVERNIGHT CHICKEN SALAD

Show ■
Go ■

1 head iceberg lettuce,
  shredded
5 c. cooked white chicken,
  cut into chunks
salt and pepper to taste
pinch of sugar
6 hard-cooked eggs, sliced
1 (8 oz.) can sliced water
  chestnuts, drained
1 sweet red onion, sliced
  and separated into rings
1 c. chopped celery
1 (10 oz.) pkg. frozen peas,
  thawed (optional)
1 pt. mayonnaise
¼ c. Durkees Famous
  Sauce
1 (8 oz.) pkg. Swiss cheese
  slices
½ c. roasted almonds

Layer all ingredients in order listed, except mayonnaise, mustard, cheese and almonds in a 9x13-inch pan. Combine mayonnaise and mustard. Spread over salad to seal. Lay strips of cheese on top. Cover tightly with foil and refrigerate overnight. Just before serving, toss in a large bowl. Add more mayonnaise if necessary. Sprinkle with almonds.

8 servings

Curry powder, chutney and capers may be added to dressing.

CHUTNEY CHICKEN SALAD

Show ■
Go ■

3 lg. cooked chicken
  breasts
½ c. Oil and Vinegar
  Dressing (see index)
½ c. chutney
1 (8 oz.) can sliced water
  chestnuts
curry powder to taste
2 green onions, chopped
mayonnaise to moisten
½ c. pignoli (pine nuts)

Marinate chicken in Dressing for a few hours. Cut into bite-size chunks. Add remaining ingredients. Sprinkle pignoli on top.

4-6 servings

May use 3 cups cooked shrimp or turkey in place of chicken.

FANTASTIC CHICKEN SALAD

Show ■
Go ☐

4 whole chicken breasts,
 boned
garlic powder
salt and pepper
2 T. oil
2 T. vinegar
2 T. orange juice
1 head romaine lettuce,
 chopped
1 head iceberg lettuce,
 chopped
1 bunch spinach, torn
1 (8 oz.) pkg. bean sprouts
4 oz. shredded Swiss
 cheese
¼ c. chopped fresh dill
3 avocados, peeled and
 quartered
1 (6 oz.) can pitted ripe
 olives, drained
1 (8 oz.) can sliced water
 chestnuts, drained
4 hard-cooked eggs,
 quartered
1 (2½ oz.) jar pimentos,
 sliced
1 red onion, sliced
fresh mushrooms (optional)

Dressing:
1 pt. mayonnaise
¼ c. chili sauce
¼ c. pickle relish
2 T. grated onion

Season chicken with garlic powder, salt and pepper. Bake at 350 degrees until tender, about 30 minutes. Cut into large chunks. Marinate in oil, vinegar and orange juice for 24 hours. When ready to serve, combine remaining salad ingredients with chicken and mix well. For dressing, combine mayonnaise, chili sauce, pickle relish and grated onion. Toss with salad.

14 servings

You may add your favorite vegetables.

Lots of ingredients, but worth it

THE NEW FRENCH CAFE
CHINESE CHICKEN SALAD

Show ■
Go □

Dressing:
8-10 cloves garlic, chopped fine
1 2-inch piece fresh ginger, chopped fine
1 c. tahini (sesame paste)
½ c. sugar
½ c. rice wine vinegar
½ c. sesame oil
1 c. Tamari soy sauce
1 T. red pepper flakes or cayenne
1-2 c. peanut oil

Salad Ingredients:
napa cabbage
radishes, thinly sliced
carrots, thinly sliced
sprigs of fresh coriander
unsalted raw peanuts, roasted
chicken breasts, skinless, boneless, poached and julienned

For dressing, combine garlic, ginger, tahini, sugar, vinegar, oil, soy sauce and red pepper flakes. With wire whisk, (not in food processor) beat in peanut oil. For salad, cut chiffonades of cabbage (sliced across in rounds). Arrange on plate. Top with radishes, carrots, coriander, peanuts and chicken. Spoon dressing on top of salad.

3 pints dressing (20 servings)

*Confucius say:
c'est magnifique!*

LE PETIT CHEF
FRESH DUCK AND PEAR SALAD

Show ■
Go ☐

1 (4 lb.) duckling
3 ripe Bartlett pears,
    peeled and halved
7 oz. Mayonnaise (see
    index)
salt and pepper
12 Boston lettuce leaves
12 ripe olives
6 radishes
1 large tomato, cut in
    wedges
2 T. blanched whole
    almonds

Roast duckling until completely cooked. Cool. Remove skin and then meat from bones. Slice pears ⅛ inch thick. Make fresh Mayonnaise. Toss sliced duckling and pears with Mayonnaise. Add seasoning to taste. Serve on a bed of Boston lettuce with garnish of ripe olives, radishes and tomato wedges. Sprinkle almonds on top. Serve very cold.

6 servings

Elegant and impressive!

BROCCOLI SALAD

Show ■
Go ■

3 bunches raw broccoli
1 c. vinegar
1 T. sugar
1 T. dill weed
1 tsp. salt
1 tsp. pepper
1 tsp. garlic salt
1½ c. vegetable oil
lettuce leaves

Make flowerets of the broccoli. Mix remaining ingredients, except lettuce leaves and pour over the broccoli. Blend well. Cover and refrigerate for 24 hours. Drain and serve on lettuce leaves or as a relish.

8-10 servings

SNOW PEA SALAD

Show ■
Go ■

¼ c. red wine vinegar
¼ c. oil
2 tsp. Dijon mustard
1 tsp. crushed garlic
1 tsp. dried dill weed
salt and pepper to taste
1 c. half and half cream
6 artichoke hearts, canned
   or frozen
2 c. thinly sliced fresh
   mushrooms
1½ c. fresh snow peas,
   trimmed and halved
½ c. sliced toasted
   almonds

Combine vinegar, oil, mustard, garlic, dill weed, salt and pepper. Pour cream into mixture in a slow stream and whisk it to blend. Toss vegetables with dressing and garnish with almonds.

4-6 servings

ROMAINE-MUSHROOM SALAD

Show ■
Go ■

¼ c. tarragon wine vinegar
2 cloves garlic, crushed
¾ c. oil
1 T. minced parsley or 2
   tsp. dill weed
1½ tsp. salt
¼ tsp. pepper
1 lb. fresh mushrooms,
   sliced
1 head romaine lettuce, cut
   up
¾ c. pitted ripe olives,
   drained
1 c. cherry tomatoes

In medium bowl, mix together vinegar, garlic, oil, parsley, salt and pepper. Add mushrooms to bowl and marinate for 1 hour. Add remaining vegetables. Toss and serve.

4-6 servings

MARINATED SALAD

Show ■
Go □

¾ c. sugar
½ c. oil
½ c. wine garlic vinegar
1 tsp. salt
½ tsp. pepper
dash red pepper
dash Tabasco
2 red or white onions,
  sliced
4 tomatoes, sliced
1 green pepper, sliced
2 radishes, sliced
2 avocados, sliced
2 cucumbers, sliced
1 (6 oz.) can ripe olives,
  sliced
1 med. head lettuce, sliced
croutons
2 hard-cooked eggs, sliced

Combine sugar, oil, vinegar, salt, pepper, red pepper and Tabasco to make marinade. Place onions, tomatoes, green pepper, radishes, avocados, cucumbers and ripe olives in a large bowl. Pour marinade over and mix well. Cover and refrigerate for 8 hours. One half hour before serving, add lettuce to vegetables; mix well. Top with croutons and eggs.

8-10 servings

CONFETTI SALAD

Show ■
Go ■

1 (17 oz.) can three bean
  salad, drained
1 (12 oz.) can whole kernel
  corn with red and green
  peppers, drained
2 green onions, thinly
  sliced or 2 slices red
  onion, separated
½ c. chopped celery
¼ c. vegetable or olive oil
¼ c. vinegar
1 T. sugar
½ tsp. salt (optional)
¼ tsp. pepper

Combine three bean salad, corn, green onions and celery in medium size bowl. Combine remaining ingredients. Stir and pour over vegetables. Toss to coat well. Cover and chill for several hours or to quick-chill, place in freezer for 30 minutes. Keeps for several days in the refrigerator.

6 servings

CHEZ COLETTE SALADE NICOISE

Show ■
Go □

7 oz. fresh green beans
10 oz. potatoes
½ head bibb lettuce
6 tomatoes, quartered
1 green pepper, cut in rings
4 ribs celery, chopped
½ cucumber, peeled and
chopped
1 (7 oz.) can tuna, drained
3 hard-cooked eggs
1 (2 oz.) can anchovies,
drained
1 (6 oz.) can ripe olives,
drained
½ c. vinegar
¾ c. olive oil
salt and pepper

In small saucepan, cook beans in water until tender. Drain and cool. In large saucepan, cook potatoes in boiling salted water. Peel, cool and slice. Line sides of serving bowl with lettuce. Place sliced potatoes in the center and green beans around the potatoes. Arrange tomatoes on top of lettuce; then green pepper. Lay celery and cucumber on top. Place tuna in center of bowl. Cut eggs in half and arrange in bowl, cut side up. Decorate salad with anchovies and olives. For dressing, mix vinegar and olive oil; add salt and pepper to taste. Pour dressing over salad and serve.

4-6 servings

BLUE HORSE CAESAR SALAD

Show ■
Go □

1 head romaine lettuce
1 clove garlic, crushed
½ tsp. freshly ground
pepper
juice of ½ lemon
1 tsp. Worcestershire sauce
1 (2 oz.) can anchovies,
chopped
1 tsp. Dijon mustard
6 T. olive oil
2 T. red wine vinegar
2 coddled eggs (boiled 1
minute)
2 T. butter
½ c. croutons
½ c. freshly grated
Parmesan cheese

Trim romaine and cut lengthwise twice and then crisscross about 1½ inches apart. Reserve. Rub crushed garlic around the bottom of a large wooden bowl. Retain pulp. Add pepper, lemon juice, Worcestershire sauce and anchovies. With a fork, mash anchovies against bottom of the bowl into a fine paste. Add mustard, olive oil and vinegar. Blend thoroughly. In small bowl, beat coddled eggs. Add and mix vigorously until dressing begins to thicken. In a shallow pan, melt butter and sauté garlic pulp until it becomes aromatic. Add croutons and sauté until lightly browned. Place romaine in wooden bowl and toss thoroughly. Add ¼ cup Parmesan cheese and croutons. Toss lightly. Serve salad on well chilled salad plates and top each portion with remaining Parmesan cheese.

6 servings

It's show time...

CAESAR SALAD

Show ■
Go ■

1 clove garlic, crushed
1 tsp. Dijon mustard
1 tsp. anchovy paste
juice of ½ lemon
2 tsp. Worcestershire sauce
1 egg
salt to taste
1 lg. head romaine lettuce
melted butter
croutons
½ c. olive oil
⅙ c. red wine vinegar
¾ c. grated Parmesan
   cheese
freshly ground pepper to
   taste

In a small bowl, mix together garlic, mustard, anchovy paste, lemon juice, Worcestershire sauce, egg and salt. Set aside.

Separate lettuce leaves and wash. Dry with a paper towel. Tear the lettuce into pieces and place in a salad bowl. In pan of melted butter, lightly brown the croutons. Pour the mixture in the small bowl and the olive oil and vinegar over the lettuce and toss lightly until mixed thoroughly. Add Parmesan cheese. Toss just enough to mix the cheese but not so the cheese becomes saturated. Add croutons, tossing once or twice. Top with freshly ground pepper and serve.

6 servings

UNPEELED POTATO SALAD

Show ■
Go ■

2½ lbs. sm. new red
   potatoes
8 hard-cooked eggs, cut in
   eighths
1-2 bunches green onions,
   chopped

Dressing:
¾ c. mayonnaise
¼ c. dairy sour cream
¼-½ c. Durkees Famous
   Sauce
1 T. dill weed
salt and pepper to taste

Wash and scrub new potatoes. Boil in large pot until tender. When potatoes are done, drain water and let cool. Cut unpeeled potatoes into cubes. Add eggs and onions. Mix with dressing and let marinate a few hours or overnight.

For dressing, mix mayonnaise, sour cream, Durkees Sauce and dill weed. Season with salt and pepper.

8-10 servings

MARINATED VEGETABLE SALAD

Show ■
Go ■

1½ c. sliced fresh
   mushrooms
1½ lbs. fresh or 2 (10 oz.)
   pkgs. frozen asparagus,
   cut in 2-inch pieces
1 (16 oz.) can garbanzos,
   drained
½ c. sliced ripe olives
½ c. sliced stuffed green
   olives
1 (9 oz.) pkg. frozen
   artichoke hearts, cooked
1 small onion, thinly sliced

Marinade:
1½ c. oil
½ c. red wine vinegar
3 T. light corn syrup
2 tsp. seasoned salt
1 tsp. basil
½ tsp. pepper

Place all salad ingredients in a large bowl. Mix marinade ingredients together in a 1-quart jar. Cover and shake well to blend. Pour marinade over salad and mix together. Cover and refrigerate overnight. When ready to serve, drain well.

8-10 servings

MARINATED SLICED TOMATOES

Show ■
Go ■

3 lg. tomatoes
⅓ c. olive oil
¼ c. red wine vinegar
1 tsp. salt
¼ tsp. pepper
½ clove garlic, crushed
2 T. finely chopped parsley
1 tsp. basil
2 T. finely chopped green
   onion
1 (4½ oz.) can sliced pitted
   ripe olives

Slice tomatoes ½-inch thick. Mix olive oil, vinegar, salt, pepper and garlic together and pour evenly over tomatoes. Sprinkle with parsley, basil, onion and olives. Cover and refrigerate 1-3 hours before serving.

4-5 servings

TORTELLINI SALAD

Show ■
Go ■

**2 (15 oz.) pkgs. frozen
  meat tortellini**
salt
drop of oil
5 green onions, chopped
**1 (2½ oz.) jar pimentos,
  drained and julienned**
**2-3 knockwurst, boiled,
  skinned and diced**
1 T. pignoli (pine nuts)

Dressing:
2 T. finely chopped dill
1 egg yolk
1 T. Dijon mustard
1 T. lemon juice
**1 T. white wine or tarragon
  vinegar**
2 T. dairy sour cream
1½ c. olive oil
salt and pepper to taste

Cook tortellini in salted boiling water with drop of oil for about 12 minutes; drain and cool thoroughly.

For dressing, combine all ingredients. Toss with tortellini. Add remaining salad ingredients and serve chilled or at room temperature.

8-10 servings

Sure company pleaser!

DELI PASTA SALAD

Show ■
Go ■

1 (12 oz.) pkg. spiral pasta
1¼ c. ripe olives
1 c. chopped green pepper
¼ lb. hard salami, cut into thin strips
1 sm. red onion, cut into rings
¼-½ c. grated Parmesan
¼ c. finely chopped parsley
1 (2½ oz.) jar pimento, drained
¾ c. Italian dressing

Cook pasta according to package directions. In large bowl, combine olives, green pepper, salami, onion, cheese, parsley, pimento and Italian dressing. Add pasta and toss well. Chill. Serve chilled or at room temperature. May be made the day before.

8-10 servings

Now, thatsa pasta!

TUNA SALAD

Show ■
Go ■

**2 (7 oz.) cans white solid
  pack tuna, drained**
**1 (11 oz.) can mandarin
  oranges, drained**
**¼ lb. fresh mushrooms,
  sliced**
**4 oz. slivered almonds,
  toasted**
**1 c. small pimento-stuffed
  green olives, cut in half**
**1 c. water-packed
  artichokes, drained**
**1 c. sliced water chestnuts,
  drained**
½ c. fried onion rings
½ c. sliced ripe olives

Dressing:
¼ c. mayonnaise
¼ c. sour cream
1 T. lemon juice
2 tsp. sugar
**1 bunch green onions,
  sliced**

Mix salad ingredients together in a large bowl. Combine dressing ingredients and mix with salad. Serve immediately.

8 servings

In tuna with the times

TARRAGON ORANGE SALAD

Show ■
Go ■

2 heads romaine lettuce
1 T. chopped parsley
2 green onions, sliced
1 (11 oz.) can mandarin
  oranges, drained
4 oz. slivered almonds
½ c. sugar

Dressing:
1 tsp. tarragon leaves
½ tsp. salt
⅛ tsp. pepper
3 tsp. sugar
½ tsp. Dijon mustard
½ c. tarragon vinegar
1 c. oil

Break lettuce in pieces; place in large bowl. Add parsley, onions and mandarin oranges. Place almonds and sugar in small saucepan over low heat until sugar dissolves and coats almonds. Remove and spread on aluminum foil to cool. For dressing, place tarragon leaves, salt, pepper, sugar and mustard in mixing bowl or food processor. Beat in vinegar. Add oil slowly and mix until light and creamy. Refrigerate 20 minutes or more before serving. Toss salad and almonds with dressing.

8 servings

STRAWBERRY ROMAINE SALAD

Show ■
Go ■

Dressing:
1 c. mayonnaise
¼ c. vinegar
⅔ c. sugar
½ c. milk
2 T. poppy seeds

1 head romaine lettuce
1 pt. fresh strawberries,
  sliced
1 Spanish onion, sliced in
  rings

Mix mayonnaise, vinegar, sugar, milk and poppy seeds. Toss with romaine, strawberries and onion.

4 servings

TROPICAL FRUIT SALAD

Show ■
Go ☐

1 (20 oz.) can pineapple
chunks
1 (11 oz.) can mandarin
oranges
1 (8 oz.) can green grapes,
drained
1-2 bananas, peeled and
sliced
1 avocado, peeled and
sliced
½ c. sugar
1 T. flour
1 egg, slightly beaten
¼ c. lemon juice

Drain and save the juice from the pineapple and oranges, separately. Combine drained fruits and add bananas and avocado. Prepare dressing by combining sugar, flour, egg, lemon juice and pineapple juice. If necessary, use reserved orange juice to make ¾ cup liquid. Mix well. Cook slowly, stirring constantly until thickened. Cool before mixing with salad fruits. Serve in lettuce-lined bowl.

6-8 servings

SUNSHINE MOLD

Show ■
Go ■

1 (6 oz.) pkg. lemon, lime
or orange flavored
gelatin
2 c. boiling water
1 (20 oz.) can crushed
pineapple
1 (8 oz.) carton Cool Whip,
thawed
1 (20 oz.) can lemon pie
filling

Dissolve gelatin in boiling water. Drain pineapple; reserve juice. Add juice to gelatin; refrigerate for 2 hours. Beat gelatin in mixer for 1 minute. Fold in Cool Whip and pie filling at slow speed. Fold in pineapple. Pour into large lightly greased gelatin mold. Refrigerate until set. To serve, unmold and surround with fresh blueberries or strawberries.

8-10 servings

May make and serve in large ungreased compote.

BASIC VINAIGRETTE DRESSING

Show ■
Go ■

1 c. oil
¼ c. red or white wine
  vinegar
½ tsp. Dijon mustard
½ tsp. chopped parsley,
  tarragon or chives
salt
freshly ground pepper

Mix all ingredients until blended.

1¼ cups

RUBY RED DRESSING

Show ■
Go ■

1 c. sugar
1 c. lemon juice
1 c. oil
1 c. ketchup
1 c. chili sauce
¼ red onion, cut up
2 cloves garlic
1 tsp. Tabasco sauce
1 tsp. Worcestershire sauce

Combine all ingredients in blender or food processor.

1 quart

JUST PLAIN SALAD DRESSING

Show ■
Go ■

½ c. oil
½ c. brown sugar
½ c. granulated sugar
1 med. onion, peeled
⅓ c. ketchup
¼ c. cider vinegar
1 tsp. Worcestershire sauce

In blender or food processor, place all ingredients in order given. Blend well. Chill and serve over your favorite green salad.

1½ pints

BLEU CHEESE DRESSING

Show ■
Go ■

2 c. mayonnaise
½ c. dairy sour cream
¼ c. tarragon vinegar
4 tsp. sugar
½ tsp. dry mustard
1 sm. clove garlic, finely
    chopped
1 green onion, white part
    only, finely chopped
4 oz. Bleu cheese,
    crumbled

Blend all ingredients, adding cheese last. Cover. Refrigerate at least 2 hours. Keeps well in refrigerator 2-3 weeks.

3 cups

So easy, you can do it all by hand!

POPPY SEED DRESSING

Show ■
Go ■

½ c. light corn syrup
1 tsp. dry mustard
1 tsp. salt
⅓ c. white vinegar
1 tsp. onion juice
dash Tabasco sauce
dash Worcestershire sauce
¼ tsp. chopped parsley
1 c. oil
½ T. poppy seeds

In blender or food processor, combine all ingredients except oil and poppy seeds. Gradually add oil until blended. Then add poppy seeds and blend again. Adjust seasonings to taste. Chill and serve. (A little sugar can be added for a sweeter dressing.)

1½ cups

SPINACH SALAD DRESSING

Show ■
Go ■

½ c. oil
1½ T. sugar
3 T. red wine vinegar
1 T. soy sauce
dash dry mustard

Combine all ingredients and mix well. Serve on your favorite spinach salad.

¾ cup

BLENDER CAESAR SALAD DRESSING

Show ■
Go ■

1 (2 oz.) can anchovies, drained
⅔ c. oil
3¾ T. lemon juice
1 tsp. Worcestershire sauce
1 tsp. Dijon mustard
ground pepper

Combine all ingredients in blender.

1 cup

Great with romaine lettuce, croutons and Parmesan cheese.

QUICK SALAD DRESSING OR MARINADE

Show ■
Go ■

⅓ c. tarragon vinegar
½ c. oil
2 tsp. salt
½ tsp. cracked pepper
2 cloves garlic, minced
1 tsp. chopped parsley (optional)

Mix in jar and refrigerate. Shake well before using.

¾ cup

Excellent marinade for mushrooms, onions, zucchini, carrots and celery or as a regular salad dressing on greens.

SEAFOOD DRESSING

Show ■
Go ■

1 (7½ oz.) can king crabmeat, shredded
⅓ c. mayonnaise
⅓ c. dairy sour cream
⅓ chili sauce

Combine ingredients in medium bowl. Cover and chill.

2 cups

Great with Egg Salad Mold (see index) or lettuce salad.

CHEZ COLETTE HOUSE DRESSING

Show ■
Go ■

3 T. mayonnaise
1 T. Dijon mustard
1 T. yellow mustard
3 T. red wine vinegar
1 tsp. salt
½ tsp. freshly ground
  pepper
½ tsp. tarragon
2 c. oil

Mix mayonnaise with mustards, vinegar and seasonings until smooth. Add the oil slowly. Adjust seasonings to taste. Add more oil if dressing is too thick.

2½ cups

This one's on the house!

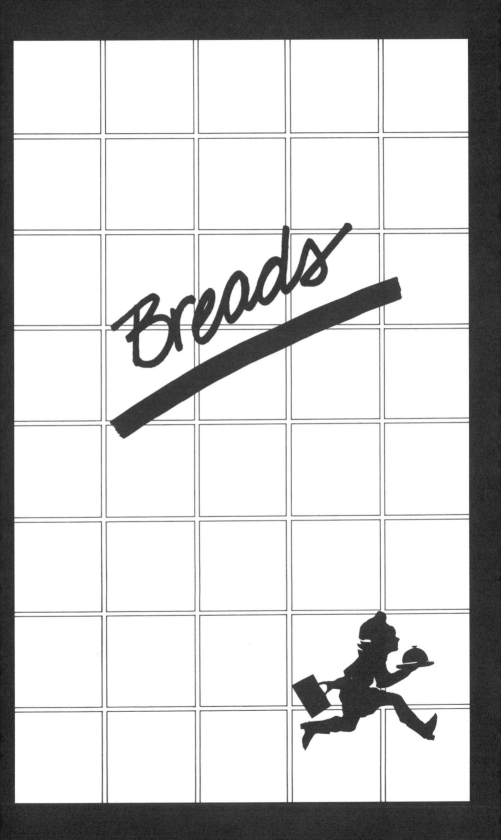

Breads

WHOLE WHEAT CHALLAH

Show ■
Go □

2 pkgs. active dry yeast
½ c. warm water
pinch of sugar
6 c. unbleached flour
2 c. whole wheat flour
1½ c. warm water
4 eggs, beaten
¾ c. safflower oil
1½ T. salt
¾ c. sugar or ¼ c. sugar
plus ¼ c. honey
1 egg, beaten with 1 T.
water
poppy or sesame seeds

Mix together yeast, ½ cup water and pinch of sugar. Set aside until dissolved and puffy. In a large bowl, mix together flours, 1½ cups water, eggs, oil, salt and sugar with hands or wooden spoon. Blend in yeast mixture. Batter will be a bit sticky. Cover bowl with warm dampened towel and set in warm place to rise.

When dough has doubled its original size, punch down and knead for 2 minutes. Cover and let rise again. After second rising, place dough on a floured surface. Divide into 2 sections. Divide each section into 3 long rolls and braid into 2 loaves. Put each loaf in a greased 5x9-inch loaf pan or on large greased cookie sheet. Let stand 20-30 minutes. Bake at 350 degrees for 15 minutes. Lightly brush tops with egg-water mixture and sprinkle with poppy or sesame seeds. Lower oven temperature to 325 degrees and continue baking for 30 minutes until brown. Remove and cool on racks. Freezes well; serve warm by reheating at 350 degrees for 10-15 minutes wrapped in foil.

2 loaves

HONEY CHALLAH

Show ■
Go □

2 pkgs. active dry yeast
4 tsp. salt
¾ c. honey
1¾ c. warm water
2 c. flour
1 c. oil
3 eggs
6-6½ c. flour
1 egg, beaten
sesame seeds

Mix yeast, salt, honey and water in large bowl. Let stand for 5 minutes. Add 2 cups flour and beat well. Blend in oil, eggs and remaining flour. Turn onto lightly floured board and knead. Place back in bowl, cover and let rise in a warm place until doubled in size, about 2-3 hours. Punch down; divide into 3 sections. Divide each section into 3 long rolls and braid into loaves. Place on cookie sheets. Cover; let rise 45 minutes. Brush with egg and sprinkle with sesame seeds. Bake at 325 degrees for 40-45 minutes.

3 small loaves

OATMEAL BREAD

Show ■
Go □

2 pkgs. active dry yeast
1 T. sugar
½ c. warm water
½ c. shortening
2 c. boiling water
1½ c. quick oatmeal
¾ c. molasses
½ c. brown sugar
¼ c. sugar
1½ tsp. salt
3 eggs, beaten
9-9½ c. flour
raisins, plumped in hot
   water (optional)

Dissolve yeast and 1 tablespoon sugar in water; let rise about 10 minutes. Meanwhile, mix together remaining ingredients except flour; cool to lukewarm. Mix part of flour in and add the yeast mixture. Add balance of flour by mixing and kneading until smooth. Raisins may be added. Let rise in a covered bowl until doubled. Shape into three loaves and place in greased 5x9-inch pans. Let rise again. Bake at 375 degrees for 45 minutes.

3 loaves

BUTTERMILK GRAHAM BREAD

Show ■
Go ■

3 c. graham whole wheat flour
2 c. unbleached flour
1 tsp. salt
2 tsp. baking soda
1 tsp. baking powder
½ c. brown sugar
2½ c. plus 2 T. buttermilk
½ c. molasses
1 c. raisins or currants, plumped in hot water

Mix dry ingredients together. Blend in liquids until moistened. Stir in raisins and pour into 2 greased 5x9-inch loaf pans. Bake at 350 degrees for 1 hour.

2 loaves

BEER BREAD

Show ■
Go ■

1 (12 oz.) can beer, room temperature
3½ c. self-rising flour
3 T. sugar

In mixing bowl, combine all ingredients by hand. Pour batter into four 3¼x5¾-inch loaf pans. Bake at 350 degrees for 1 hour.

4 mini loaves

EXTRA TERRIFIC BREAD LOAF

Show ■
Go ■

1 loaf French bread
1 c. butter, softened
¾ T. dry mustard
2 T. poppy seed
2½ T. finely chopped green onion
1 (8 oz.) pkg. Swiss cheese, cut diagonally to form triangles
1 med. onion, thinly sliced

Remove side crust from bread. Slice 16 pieces ¾ way through to bottom crust. Mix together butter, mustard, poppy seed and green onion. Blend well. Spread mixture between slices, saving some for top and sides of loaf. Place 1 cheese triangle and 1 onion ring in each slit between pieces. Spread top and sides with remaining butter. Wrap in foil. Heat at 325 degrees for 20-30 minutes or until cheese has melted. Open foil last 10 minutes to brown.

16 servings

POPPY SEED BREAD

Show ■
Go ■

2½ c. sugar
2½ c. oil
2 c. evaporated milk
5 eggs
½ c. milk
5 c. flour
4½ tsp. baking powder
¼ tsp. salt
½ c. poppy seeds
2½ tsp. vanilla

In electric mixer bowl, combine sugar, oil, evaporated milk, eggs and milk; beat at medium speed. Mix well. Sift together flour, baking powder and salt; slowly blend into creamed mixture. Add poppy seeds and vanilla; mix until smooth. Pour batter into two generously greased 5x9-inch loaf pans. Bake at 350 degrees for 55 minutes, until golden brown.

2 loaves

A sweet quick bread that may be baked as muffins; reduce baking time to 30 minutes.

CARROT COCONUT BREAD

Show ■
Go ■

3 eggs
½ c. oil
1 tsp. orange or lemon
   extract
2 c. finely shredded carrots
2 c. shredded coconut
1 c. raisins
1 c. chopped pecans
2 c. flour
½ tsp. salt
1 tsp. baking soda
1 tsp. baking powder
1 tsp. cinnamon
1 c. sugar

In large bowl, beat eggs until light. Stir in oil and extract. Add carrots, coconut, raisins and nuts. Mix well. Combine flour, salt, baking soda, baking powder, cinnamon and sugar. Stir into first mixture until blended. Spoon mixture into a greased and floured 5x9-inch loaf pan. Bake at 350 degrees for 1 hour or until browned. Remove from pan and cool. Wrap in foil and refrigerate overnight. May be frozen.

1 loaf

ZUCCHINI NUT BREAD

Show ■
Go ■

3 c. flour
2 tsp. cinnamon
1 tsp. baking soda
1 tsp. salt
¾ tsp. baking powder
1 T. grated lemon rind
2 c. grated, unpeeled
　zucchini
1 c. chopped walnuts
1¾ c. sugar
1 c. oil
4 eggs
⅛ tsp. lemon juice

Blend together flour, cinnamon, baking soda, salt and baking powder. Set aside. In medium bowl, combine lemon rind, zucchini and walnuts; set aside. In large mixing bowl, combine sugar, oil, eggs and lemon juice; beat until smooth. Add dry ingredients and mix well. Stir in zucchini mixture and combine. Divide batter evenly between two greased and floured 5x9-inch loaf pans. Bake at 350 degrees for 55-60 minutes or until cake tester comes out clean. Cool in pan 10 minutes; remove and cool completely. Cut in thin slices.

2 loaves

STRAWBERRY BREAD

Show ■
Go ■

3 c. flour
1 tsp. baking powder
1 tsp. baking soda
1 tsp. salt
2 tsp. cinnamon
2 c. sugar
4 eggs, well beaten
1¼ c. oil
2 (10 oz.) pkgs. frozen
　strawberries, thawed
1¼ c. chopped pecans
¼ c. strawberry jam

Mix together flour, baking powder, baking soda, salt, cinnamon and sugar. Add eggs, oil, strawberries, pecans and jam. Blend. Pour batter into 2 well greased 5x9-inch loaf pans. Bake at 350 degrees for 1 hour.

2 loaves

BANANA CHOCOLATE CHIP LOAF

Show ■
Go ■

3 ripe bananas
½ c. butter or margarine,
  melted
1 c. sugar
2 eggs
1 tsp. vanilla
2 c. flour
1 tsp. baking soda
¼ tsp. salt
¾ c. chocolate chips
powdered sugar

In food processor or blender, combine bananas, butter, sugar, eggs and vanilla. Blend well. Add flour, soda and salt. Fold in chocolate chips. Pour batter into a greased 5x9-inch loaf pan. Bake at 350 degrees for 1 hour. Cool and remove from pan. Sprinkle with powdered sugar. Wrap tightly in foil. This loaf is better the second day. Freezes well.

1 loaf

HEALTH NUT BANANA BREAD

Show □
Go ■

½ c. chopped walnuts
2 c. flour
1 tsp. baking powder
1 tsp. baking soda
½ c. corn oil margarine
½ c. sugar
1 c. mashed banana (3 sm.
  or 2 med.)
3 T. skim milk
1 tsp. vanilla
½ c. golden raisins or
  chopped dates

Toast walnuts in 350 degree oven for 10 minutes. Blend together flour, baking powder and baking soda; set aside. Cream margarine and sugar. Add bananas, milk and vanilla. Mix well. Blend in dry ingredients. Stir in nuts and raisins. Pour batter into a greased 5x9-inch loaf pan. Bake at 350 degrees for 55 minutes or until top is golden brown and firm.

1 loaf

This is an eggless banana bread.

a top banana!

CRANBERRY ORANGE BREAD

Show ■
Go ■

2 c. flour
1 c. sugar
1½ tsp. baking powder
½ tsp. salt
½ tsp. baking soda
2 T. butter, softened
¾ c. orange juice
1 egg
1 c. raw cranberries, cut in
   half
½ c. chopped nuts
   (optional)

In large bowl place dry ingredients. Add butter, juice and egg; mix well. Fold in cranberries and nuts. Pour into greased 5x9-inch loaf pan. Bake at 350 degrees for 50 minutes. Cool 5 minutes and remove from pan.

1 loaf

MACADAMIA NUT LOAF

Show ■
Go ■

1 c. unsalted butter,
   softened
2 c. sugar
4 eggs
1 c. mashed banana
4 c. flour
2 tsp. baking powder
1 tsp. baking soda
½ tsp. salt
1 (15½ oz.) can crushed
   pineapple, undrained
1 c. shredded coconut
1 c. chopped macadamia
   nuts

Beat butter and sugar together thoroughly. Add eggs and mix well. Stir in bananas. Add flour, baking powder, baking soda and salt to creamed mixture. Fold in pineapple, coconut and nuts. Pour into 2 greased 5x9-inch loaf pans. Bake at 350 degrees for 65-70 minutes.

2 loaves

APRICOT NUT BREAD

Show ■
Go ■

8 oz. chopped dates
1½ c. chopped dried
  apricots
2 tsp. baking soda
1½ c. sugar
8 T. butter
1¾ c. apricot nectar,
  boiling
2 eggs, slightly beaten
2½ c. flour
1 c. chopped nuts

In large bowl, combine dates, apricots, soda, sugar and butter. Cover with boiling apricot nectar. When cool, add eggs, flour and nuts. Mix well. Pour into two greased 8x4-inch loaf pans. Bake at 350 degrees for 55-60 minutes.

2 loaves

HEALTHY MUFFINS

Show ■
Go ■

1-15 oz. box raisin bran
½ c. raisins or chopped
  dates
3 c. natural sugar
5 c. flour
1 tsp. salt
2 T. baking soda
4 eggs, beaten
1 qt. buttermilk
1 c. oil
2 T. vanilla
¾ c. unprocessed bran
½ c. wheat germ

In large bowl mix together raisin bran, raisins or dates, sugar, flour, salt, soda, eggs, buttermilk, oil and vanilla. Gently stir in the bran and wheat germ. Do not overstir. Spoon into greased muffin tins. Bake at 400 degrees for 15-20 minutes.

tons of muffins

For miniature muffin tins bake only 10-15 minutes. Batter keeps up to 6 weeks in refrigerator.

"*Take two and call me in the morning*"

SWEDISH KRINGLE

Show ■
Go ■

Dough:
½ c. butter
1 c. flour
1 T. water

Filling:
½ c. butter
1 c. water
1 c. flour
3 eggs
½ tsp. almond extract

Icing:
2 c. powdered sugar
milk
½ tsp. almond extract

sliced almonds

Combine ½ cup butter, 1 cup flour and 1 tablespoon water. Mix to consistency of pie crust; pat into 2 oblong shapes about 4 inches wide on a lightly greased cookie sheet. Bring to a boil ½ cup butter, 1 cup water and quickly stir in 1 cup flour and the eggs, one at a time. Add ½ teaspoon almond extract. Spread mixture over dough on cookie sheet. Bake at 375 degrees for 45 minutes. Remove from oven and cool.

For icing, add enough milk to powdered sugar until it is of spreading consistency; add ½ teaspoon almond extract. Spread on kringles. Sprinkle top with almonds; slice and serve.

2 kringles

BLUEBERRY COFFEE CAKE

Show ■
Go ■

¼ c. butter
¾ c. sugar
1 egg
2 c. flour
2 tsp. baking powder
½ tsp. salt
½ c. milk
1 scant pt. blueberries,
    washed, drained and
    lightly dusted with flour

Streusel:
¼ c. flour
¼ c. sugar
2 T. butter

Cream ¼ c. butter and ¾ cup sugar. Add egg. Sift together 2 cups flour, baking powder and salt. Add dry ingredients to creamed mixture alternately with milk. Fold in blueberries. Pour batter into a greased 5x9-inch loaf pan. Combine ¼ cup flour, ¼ cup sugar and 2 tablespoons butter until crumbly and sprinkle over batter. Bake at 350 degrees for 1 hour.

1 loaf

CHOCOLATE CHIP COFFEE CAKE

Show ■
Go ■

½ c. butter, softened
1 c. sugar
½ tsp. salt
2 eggs, slightly beaten
2 c. flour
1 tsp. baking powder
1 tsp. baking soda
1 c. dairy sour cream
1 tsp. vanilla

Streusel:
½ c. sugar
1 tsp. cinnamon
¾ c. chocolate chips
½ c. brown sugar
½ c. chopped nuts
  (optional)

In mixer bowl, cream butter and sugar. Add salt, eggs and mix well. Sift together flour, baking powder and baking soda. Add to creamed mixture alternately with the sour cream. Add vanilla.

For streusel, combine sugar, cinnamon, chocolate chips, brown sugar and nuts. Spread half of the cake batter in a greased 9x9-inch pan. Sprinkle with half of streusel mixture. Spread remaining cake batter on top and sprinkle with remaining streusel mixture. Bake at 350 degrees for 35-40 minutes. When toothpick comes out clean, cake is done.

As a variation a 10-inch tube pan can be used. Cool upright for 15 minutes, invert to remove and turn streusel side up on serving platter.

16-20 pieces

Good morning, Mr. Chips!

MARBLEIZED COFFEE CAKE

Show ■
Go ■

4 eggs, well beaten
¾ c. oil
¾ c. water
1 tsp. vanilla
1 T. butter extract
1 (1.4 oz.) envelope
   whipped topping mix
1 (3⅝ oz.) pkg. instant
   vanilla pudding mix
1 (#2 Deluxe) Duncan Hines
   yellow cake mix

Streusel:
¼ c. sugar
2 tsp. cinnamon
¼ c. chopped pecans

Glaze:
¾ c. powdered sugar,
   sifted
1½ T. milk
1 tsp. vanilla
1 tsp. butter extract

chopped pecans

Combine eggs, oil, water, vanilla and butter extract in large mixing bowl. Add whipped topping mix, pudding mix and cake mix. Beat 7 minutes. Grease a 15x4x4-inch or two 9x5-inch loaf pans and pour in ¾ of batter.

For streusel, combine sugar, cinnamon and pecans; sprinkle on top of batter in pan. Pour remaining batter over streusel mixture. With a knife, swirl through batter to marbleize. Bake at 350 degrees for 50-60 minutes. Cake is done when toothpick inserted in center comes out clean. Let cool before removing from pan. For glaze, combine sugar, milk, vanilla and butter extract. Pour glaze over cake and sprinkle with pecans.

24 slices

Place in the oven and see what developps

CARAMEL PECAN ROLLS

Show ■
Go □

1 cake yeast (.02 oz.)
½ c. warm water
1 c. milk
½ c. sugar
1 tsp. salt
2 eggs, slightly beaten
1 c. butter
4 c. flour
1 c. butter
1 c. brown sugar
1 tsp. cinnamon

Syrup:
1½ c. brown sugar
1½ c. butter
4½ T. honey

2 (8 oz.) pkgs. whole
   pecans

Dissolve yeast in warm water. Scald milk; add sugar and salt. Cool to lukewarm. Add eggs to milk mixture and combine with yeast. In separate bowl, cut 1 cup butter into flour until pea size. Add one-half of yeast mixture. Mix well. Add remaining mixture and blend. Cover and refrigerate overnight.

Next day, separate dough into two pieces. Roll 1 piece into 11x18-inch rectangle. Melt 1 cup butter and brush surface generously then sprinkle with mixture of brown sugar and cinnamon. Roll up jelly roll fashion, tightly sealing edges, and cut into 18 pieces. Repeat for second piece.

To make syrup, mix brown sugar, butter and honey together; boil 2 minutes. Preheat oven to 180 degrees. Pour syrup evenly into ungreased muffin tins. Place 3 or 4 pecan halves on top of syrup and place roll in tin cut side up. Cover with clean dish towels. Turn off oven. Place the tins on cookie sheets in oven for 30 minutes; remove.

Re-heat oven to 375 degrees; remove towels and bake rolls 25-35 minutes. Remove from oven and place a cookie sheet over tins and turn upside down. Do not take the tins off the rolls for 1 minute. Tap gently and remove tins. Let cool.

36 rolls

PETITE CARAMEL ROLLS

Show ■
Go ■

2 c. butter or margarine,
  softened
16 oz. sm. curd cottage
  cheese
3½ c. flour
½ c. sugar plus 1 tsp.
  cinnamon
½ c. butter, melted
½ c. brown sugar
¼ c. chopped pecans

Blend together butter, cottage cheese and flour to form a smooth dough. Divide into 4 parts. Wrap each ball separately in floured waxed paper. Refrigerate a few hours or overnight. Roll one ball at a time to about a 5x12-inch rectangle, ⅛-inch thick. Sprinkle with cinnamon-sugar mixture and roll up dough starting with long side. Place ½ teaspoon butter, ½ teaspoon brown sugar and ¼ teaspoon pecans in bottom of each small muffin cup. Cut dough into 1-inch slices and place in muffin cup cut side up. Bake at 375 degrees for 35-40 minutes or until brown.

4 dozen

NEW ENGLAND BRAN MUFFINS

Show ■
Go ■

1 c. pure bran
1 c. water
1 c. flour
¼ c. brown sugar
½ tsp. salt
½ tsp. baking soda
1½ tsp. baking powder
1 egg
3 T. honey
¼ c. oil
½ c. chopped dates
½ c. chopped nuts
  (optional)

Soak bran in water. Mix together flour, sugar, salt, baking soda and baking powder. Add egg, honey, oil and bran. Stir only to moisten. Add dates and nuts. Spoon into greased muffin tins. Bake at 400 degrees for 20 minutes.

12 muffins

May use half whole wheat flour.

PERFECT POPOVERS

Show ■
Go ■

6 eggs
½ c. milk
½ c. water
¼ c. oil
1 c. flour
½ tsp. salt
grated Parmesan cheese
   (optional)

Beat eggs, milk, water and oil by hand or slow speed on mixer. Add flour and salt. Mix at medium speed until smooth. Preheat oven to 450 degrees. Heat popover pans or individual custard cups on cookie sheet for 15 minutes. Remove from oven and coat with oil. Dust the pans with Parmesan cheese, if desired. Fill each cup ½ to ¾ full. Bake at 450 degrees for 30 minutes. Reduce heat to 300 degrees and bake 15 minutes more.

10 popovers

POPPY SEED SCONES

Show ■
Go ■

½ c. butter
2 T. sugar
2 eggs, beaten
¾ c. dairy sour cream
2 c. flour
1 T. baking powder
1 T. poppy seeds

Using pastry blender, cut butter into sugar until crumbly. Mix eggs and sour cream and add to mixture. Add flour, baking powder and poppy seeds; mix well. Place on floured board, roll into 12-inch circle and cut into 12 wedges. Place on greased cookie sheet. Bake at 450 degrees for 15 minutes.

12 scones

BRIOCHE

⅓ c. warm water
1 pkg. active dry yeast
1½ T. sugar
¼ tsp. salt
⅔ c. butter, softened
4 lg. eggs
3 c. flour
1 egg yolk
2 tsp. water

The night before, place water in a large electric mixer bowl and sprinkle with yeast. Add sugar and salt; stir. Beat in butter, eggs and 2 cups flour for 4 minutes on medium speed. Add remaining 1 cup flour and beat at low speed for 1 minute. Cover with buttered waxed paper and damp towel. Let rise in warm place until doubled, about 2½ hours. Punch down; cover bowl again with buttered waxed paper and damp towel. Refrigerate overnight.

The next day, grease a 5-cup brioche mold with shortening, not butter. Pinch off ⅙ of dough and roll into a small ball. Knead rest of dough for 1 minute until smooth. Form an oval shape and place in brioche mold. Make an indentation in center of dough and insert rolled ball. Cover and let rise until doubled, about 2 hours. Mix together egg yolk and water. Brush top. Cover loosely with foil and bake at 375 degrees for 20 minutes. Remove foil and bake 30-40 minutes longer or until golden brown. Watch carefully. To test, tap top of bread; if it sounds hollow it's done. Remove from oven and let cool for 20 minutes in pan.

1 large bread

This can also be baked in a greased 2-pound coffee can. Voilá!

Voilá!

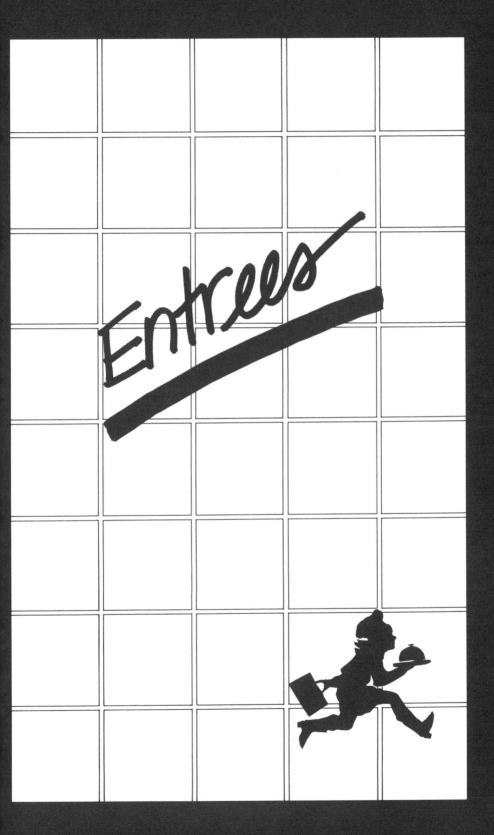

IN-THE-OVEN ITALIAN STEW

Show ■
Go ■

2 lbs. chuck roast, cubed
2 onions, quartered
4 potatoes, peeled and
    quartered
2 carrots, peeled and
    quartered
¼ c. dry Italian flavored
    bread crumbs
½ tsp. salt
1 tsp. basil
1 tsp. oregano
1 tsp. thyme
1 (16 oz.) can tomatoes
    with juice
¾ c. dry red wine
1 tsp. Worcestershire sauce
½ (10 oz.) pkg. frozen
    baby peas, thawed
½ lb. fresh mushrooms,
    sliced

In a large casserole, combine all ingredients except peas and mushrooms. Cover and bake at 325 degrees for 3 hours. Add remaining vegetables and bake uncovered for another 30-40 minutes.

4-6 servings

May omit potatoes and serve over buttered noodles or rice.

BARBECUED BRISKET

Show ■
Go ■

1 (5-7 lb.) beef brisket
3 cloves garlic, slivered
pepper and paprika to
    taste
1 c. honey
1½-2 c. ketchup
1 envelope dry onion soup
    mix
3-5 drops liquid smoke
1 T. soy sauce

Make slits on top of brisket, insert garlic slivers and place in large roasting pan. Season with pepper and paprika. Combine honey, ketchup, onion soup, liquid smoke and soy sauce; cook over low heat until blended. Pour sauce over brisket. Seal pan with foil and bake at 325 degrees for 4 hours. Remove foil last 30 minutes to brown.

6-8 servings

SWEET AND SOUR BRISKET

Show ■
Go ■

1 (5½ lb.) beef brisket
Lawry's seasoned salt
onion salt
pepper
garlic powder
1 qt. sauerkraut, drained
1½ c. brown sugar
3 c. tomato juice
¾ c. ketchup

Season brisket with salts, pepper and garlic powder. Place in roasting pan and surround with sauerkraut. Top with brown sugar and tomato juice. Bake covered at 325 degrees for 3 hours. Add ketchup and uncover last 30 minutes.

6-8 servings

CHILI CON CARNE

Show □
Go ■

2 lbs. ground beef
1 med. onion, chopped
2 cloves garlic, crushed
1 (15 oz.) can tomato sauce
1 (12 oz.) can tomato paste
1 (12 oz.) can water
2 tsp. salt
¼ tsp. freshly ground
   pepper
¾ tsp. ground cumin
3-4 T. chili powder
dash Tabasco
2 (15½ oz.) cans kidney
   beans

Brown beef, onion and garlic. Drain off excess fat. Stir in remaining ingredients except beans. Simmer 30-45 minutes. Stir in beans and heat another 10 minutes. Adjust seasoning. Cool and refrigerate. Reheat next day.

6 servings

Best made day before. Tabasco gets hotter as it blends with chili so start out with a dash and add more if needed.

For a "chili" day ... Brrr

CHICAGO STYLE PIZZAS

Show ■
Go □

Filling (prepare night before):
2 lbs. ground beef
2 cloves garlic, crushed
1 tsp. oregano
1 tsp. basil
pinch of sugar
¼ tsp. fennel seed

Dough:
2 pkgs. active dry yeast
¾ tsp. sugar
¼ c. water
4 c. flour
¼ c. oil
½ tsp. salt
9 oz. beer, room temperature

Topping:
salt
1 c. grated Parmesan cheese
2 lbs. Mozzarella cheese
2 (28 oz.) cans whole tomatoes, drained and coarsley chopped
oregano
basil
salt
pepper
grated Parmesan cheese

In a large bowl, mix together all filling ingredients. Cover tightly and refrigerate. For dough, combine yeast, sugar and water in a small bowl. Stir and let set until it doubles in size, about 10 minutes. In a large bowl, combine the yeast mixture with the flour, oil, salt and beer. Knead until smooth. Let dough rise about 2 hours. Divide dough into 4 balls. Roll each ball ¼ inch thick and place in 4 ungreased 8-inch cake pans. Edges should be ¾ inch up the sides of the pans. Salt the dough in the pans and sprinkle with Parmesan cheese.

Place one layer of Mozzarella cheese on top, and cover with about 4 tomatoes. Sprinkle with heavy shakes of oregano, basil, salt and pepper. Cover with meat mixture and press down with back of spoon. Top with heavy shakes of Parmesan cheese. Bake at 450 degrees for 30-35 minutes. Watch carefully. Cut and serve hot.

For freezing bake for 18-20 minutes and then freeze. When needed, reheat for about 30 minutes.

Four 8-inch pizzas

May also add sliced mushrooms, onions, ripe olives, green pepper, anchovies or whatever suits your pizza.

TOSTADO PIZZA

Show ■
Go □

2 T. yellow cornmeal
2 c. Bisquick
½ c. cold water
1 lb. ground beef
¾ c. water
3 T. chopped green chilies
  or green pepper
1 (6¼ oz.) pkg. taco
  seasoning mix
1 (15½ oz.) can refried
  beans
2½ c. shredded Cheddar
  cheese
fresh chili peppers
  (optional)
1 c. shredded lettuce
1 c. chopped tomato
½ c. chopped onion
taco sauce

Generously grease a 12-inch pizza pan. Sprinkle with cornmeal. In large bowl combine Bisquick and ½ c. cold water. Stir with fork until dough follows fork around the bowl. Turn out on lightly floured surface. Knead 5 or 6 times. Roll to 14-inch circle and pat into prepared pizza pan. Crimp edges.

In skillet, brown meat; drain off fat. Add ¾ cup water, green chilies and taco seasoning mix; bring to a boil. Reduce heat and simmer uncovered for 15 minutes or until mixture is thick. Spread refried beans on dough. Spread meat mixture evenly over the beans.

Bake at 450 degrees for 18-20 minutes. Sprinkle with Cheddar cheese. Return to oven about 4 minutes or until cheese is melted. Cut and garnish with fresh peppers. Pass lettuce, tomato, onion and taco sauce.

6 slices

The best of two worlds

HOT MEXICAN LASAGNE

Show ■
Go ■

1½ lbs. ground beef
1 med. onion, chopped
1½ tsp. ground cumin
2 cloves garlic, crushed
3 tsp. chili powder
1½ tsp. salt
½ tsp. pepper
¾ c. water
2 c. hot taco sauce
12 corn tortillas
1 lb. Monterey Jack cheese, shredded
1 (8 oz.) carton dairy sour cream

In large skillet, sauté beef and onion, stirring occasionally. Drain off drippings and add all seasonings and water. Simmer uncovered, stirring occasionally until most liquid has evaporated, about 10 minutes.

Pour ½ cup taco sauce into greased 9x13 baking dish. Arrange half of the tortillas to cover the bottom of the pan. Pour ½ cup taco sauce evenly over tortillas. Spoon on all of beef mixture; top with sour cream applied in even "dollops" over the beef. Sprinkle with ½ of shredded cheese. Arrange remaining tortillas, overlapping slightly, on cheese. Spread remaining taco sauce over tortillas and top with rest of cheese. Cover with foil and bake at 375 degrees for 40 minutes. Remove foil and bake 5 more minutes. Let casserole stand for 5 minutes before eating.

8-10 servings

Some like it "not hot" so use mild taco sauce.

SPICY BEEF AND PEANUTS

Show ■
Go ■

1 lb. flank steak, sliced into 2x¼-inch strips

Marinade:
1 T. dark soy sauce
1 T. cornstarch
1 T. oil

Sauce:
1 tsp. cornstarch
1 T. dry sherry
1½ T. dark soy sauce
2 tsp. red wine vinegar
2 tsp. sugar
1 tsp. sesame oil

2 c. oil
2-4 dried chili peppers, to taste
3 slices peeled gingerroot (size of a quarter) finely chopped
½ c. unsalted peanuts
1 green onion, sliced

Place beef in bowl with marinade made of soy sauce, cornstarch and oil. Refrigerate 30 minutes. Combine sauce ingredients and set aside.

One hour before serving, heat 2 cups oil in wok over high heat. Add meat and fry quickly 2 minutes or until no longer pink. Drain and let cool. Reheat wok and add 2 tablespoons oil; reduce heat. Add chili peppers and press into oil until they darken. Add ginger and stir. Increase heat and stir fry meat with spicy oil. Mix sauce well and pour over meat until evenly coated. Add peanuts. To serve, garnish with sliced green onion.

3-4 servings

Sliced chicken breasts instead of beef are a nice change.

This gets raves!

PSEUDO PRAKAS

Show ■
Go ■

1 med. cabbage, shredded
3 lbs. ground beef
1 jumbo or 2 small eggs
1 c. bread crumbs
2 tsp. salt
⅛ tsp. garlic powder
freshly ground pepper
1 (10 oz.) bottle chili sauce
½-⅔ c. water
1 (16 oz.) can whole
  cranberries
1 (8 oz.) can tomato sauce
  (optional)

Place cabbage in large roasting pan. Combine meat, eggs, bread crumbs, salt, garlic powder and pepper; shape into small balls. Place on top of cabbage. Mix chili sauce, water, cranberries and tomato sauce together; pour over meatballs. Cover and bake at 350 degrees for 3 hours. Excellent frozen and reheated.

8 servings

MEAT LOAF WELLINGTON

Show ■
Go ☐

4 lbs. ground beef
2 eggs
½ c. ketchup
½ envelope dry onion soup
  mix
salt and pepper
1 tsp. garlic powder
¼-½ c. grated Parmesan
  cheese
¼-½ c. Italian flavored
  bread crumbs
1 (2½ oz.) jar sliced
  mushrooms, drained
1 c. shredded Cheddar
  cheese
2 pre-rolled Pepperidge
  Farm puff pastry sheets,
  thawed
1 egg, beaten
1 T. water

Mix together meat, eggs, ketchup, onion soup, salt, pepper, garlic powder, Parmesan cheese and bread crumbs. Bake in 2 ungreased 5x9-inch loaf pans at 350 degrees for 30 minutes. Line a jelly roll pan with foil. Drain off juice from baked meat loaves; invert loaves on jelly roll pan. Top meat loaves with mushrooms and Cheddar cheese; pat down well. Roll out pastry sheets and place on top of the loaves. Make sure sides are well covered. Brush tops with egg and water mixture. Bake at 400 degrees for 30-35 minutes or until nicely browned. Loaves may be frozen.

10 servings

VARIATIONS ON A THEME

BEEF TENDERLOIN VARIATION I

Show ■
Go ■

1 (3½-4 lb.) whole beef
   tenderloin
2 T. butter or margarine
¼ c. chopped green onions
2 T. butter
2 T. soy sauce
1 tsp. Dijon mustard
freshly ground pepper
¾ c. sherry

Spread tenderloin with 2 tablespoons butter. Place on a rack in a shallow baking pan. Bake uncovered at 400 degrees for 15 minutes. Meanwhile, in a small saucepan, cook green onions in 2 tablespoons butter until tender. Add soy sauce, mustard and pepper. Stir in sherry and heat just to boiling. Pour over tenderloin and bake 15-20 minutes for rare to medium beef. Baste several times with sauce. Extra sauce may be passed.

10-12 servings

BEEF TENDERLOIN VARIATION II

Show ■
Go ■

1 (3½-4 lb.) whole beef
   tenderloin
Jane's Krazy Mixed-up Salt
ketchup
butter or margarine

Season beef to taste. Pour ketchup on top of roast, just until it begins to drip down the sides. Place large chunks of butter on top, every 2-3 inches. Amount of butter is dependent on size of meat. Be generous! Ketchup and butter will caramelize during baking. Bake at 425 degrees for 25-35 minutes depending on the size of the meat. This dish is best served rare or medium rare.

10-12 servings

BEEF TENDERLOIN VARIATION III

Show ■
Go ■

1 (3½-4 lb.) whole beef
   tenderloin
salt and pepper
garlic powder
Lawry's seasoned salt
lemon pepper
soy sauce
Worcestershire sauce
1 (8 oz.) bottle Caesar
   salad dressing

Generously season tenderloin with salt, pepper, garlic powder, seasoned salt and lemon pepper. Sprinkle with soy sauce and Worcestershire. Pour dressing over meat and marinate in refrigerator overnight. Before cooking, drain off marinade. Bake at 450 degrees for 20-30 minutes, depending on size of meat.

10-12 servings

SPANISH TONGUE

Show ■
Go □

1 (2½-3 lb.) fresh tongue
½ tsp. salt
½ tsp. pepper
3 whole cloves
½ tsp. cinnamon
½ tsp. nutmeg
3 celery tops
½ med. onion
3 ribs celery, sliced
3 carrots, peeled and
   sliced
1 med. onion, chopped
2 tsp. butter
1 (10½ oz.) pkg. frozen
   peas, thawed
1 (10½ oz.) can tomato
   soup
2 tsp. brown sugar

Place tongue in large pot and cover with water. Add salt, pepper, cloves, cinnamon, nutmeg, celery tops and ½ onion; simmer until tender, about 3 hours. Remove tongue; partially cool and remove skin. Save and strain liquid. Lightly sauté the celery, carrots and chopped onion in butter. Add peas. Cut tongue in thin slices and add to vegetables. Add tomato soup, 2-3 cups strained liquid and brown sugar; simmer uncovered 30 minutes or bake in casserole at 325 degrees for 45 minutes. Serve with broad noodles or rice.

4-6 servings

Try adding canned mushrooms, sautéed green pepper or canned corn niblets.

CHICKEN BREAST WITH MUSTARD PERSILLADE

Show ■
Go ■

4 whole boned chicken breasts, cut in half
½ c. Dijon mustard

Persillade Coating:
½ c. butter
4 cloves garlic, crushed
2 c. bread crumbs (2 slices fresh bread)
⅔ c. minced parsley, firmly packed
salt and pepper

Rinse chicken under cold water and pat dry with paper towels. Place on large sheet of waxed paper. Brush skin side of each breast generously with mustard. To make persillade coating, sauté garlic in butter. Add crumbs and stir over medium heat until lightly browned. Mix in parsley and season to taste.

Carefully dip mustard sides into persillade and press firmly to make crumbs adhere. Place chicken breasts, crumb side up, in a baking dish. Bake at 425 degrees for 25-30 minutes or until persillade coating is golden brown.

4-6 servings

Keep left over persillade refrigerated in airtight container for up to five days. May be frozen.

What's Persillade?
Try it, you'll like it!

CHICKEN CHINESE

Show ■
Go ■

4 whole boned chicken breasts
1 (8 oz.) bottle Italian dressing
Jane's Krazy Mixed-up Salt
garlic powder
paprika
2 c. fried rice
1 (9½ oz.) jar sweet and sour sauce

Marinate chicken breasts in dressing overnight. Next day drain and season chicken with salt, garlic powder and paprika to taste. Place 1 heaping teaspoon of fried rice in center of each breast. Roll up and secure with toothpick. Place in 9x13-inch baking dish. Bake at 350 degrees for 20 minutes. If skin is not crisp, place under broiler until golden brown and crisp. Pour sweet and sour sauce to cover chicken breasts. Bake 20 minutes more or until tender. Large chicken breasts may take longer.

4-6 servings

Remaining rice may be served on the side.

THE PLANNERS CHICKEN DIJONNAISE

Show ■
Go ■

4 (6 oz.) chicken breasts, boned, skinned and pounded
Dijon mustard
flour
3 T. butter
¼ c. dry white wine
1 c. whipping cream
1 T. Dijon mustard
salt and pepper

Spread chicken breasts lightly on both sides with mustard. Dredge in flour and shake off excess. Brown in butter over medium heat on both sides about 4-5 minutes per side. Remove to a heatproof platter and keep warm. Pour wine into skillet and boil rapidly, scraping up brown bits. Add cream and boil 2-3 minutes or until slightly thickened. Stir in 1 tablespoon mustard, salt and pepper to taste. Pour over chicken and serve.

4 servings

CHICKEN MADEIRA

Show ■
Go □

4 whole boned chicken
  breasts, skinned and cut
  in half
salt and pepper
garlic powder
½ c. flour
¼ c. butter
Madeira Sauce:
½ c. butter
1 T. chopped onion
1 T. chopped celery
1 clove garlic, crushed
⅓ c. flour
2 (10½ oz.) cans beef
  broth plus ¼ c. water
2 oz. Madeira wine
1 oz. brandy
4-6 c. cooked wild rice
fresh parsley

Season chicken with salt, pepper and garlic powder to taste. Dredge in flour, shaking off excess. Sauté in ¼ cup butter until golden brown; set aside.

For Madeira sauce, melt ½ cup butter in large skillet to foaming consistency. Add onion, celery, garlic and sauté for about 5 minutes. Blend in flour and add beef broth, wine and brandy. Cover, bring to a boil and simmer about 30 minutes. Strain and check seasonings.

Cut chicken pieces in half and place in hot Madeira sauce until chicken is heated through and coated with sauce. Place chicken pieces over rice and garnish with fresh parsley.

4-6 servings

Lobster can be used along with chicken.

COMPANY CHICKEN

Show ■
Go ▨

6 whole chicken breasts
¼ c. butter, melted
salt and pepper to taste
garlic powder
2 (10¾ oz.) cans cream of
  chicken soup
¾ c. Sauterne wine
¼ c. water
4 oz. fresh mushrooms,
  sliced
1 (8 oz.) can sliced water
  chestnuts
¾ c. green grapes
1 c. chopped parsley

Brush chicken with butter and season well with salt, pepper and garlic powder. Broil until brown, about 10 minutes per side; place in 9x13-inch baking pan. Combine soup, wine and water and pour over chicken. Cover with remaining ingredients. Bake covered at 350 degrees for 1 hour. Uncover to brown last 15 minutes.

6 servings

CHICKEN MARAKESH

Show ■
Go □

8 lbs. cut-up chicken
seasoned salt
2 c. cornflake crumbs
½ c. butter
3 onions, sliced
1 (2¼ oz.) can sliced ripe
  olives
1 lb. fresh mushrooms,
  sliced
½ c. golden raisins
1 (16 oz.) can tomatoes
1½ c. white wine
2 c. white rice, cooked

Season chicken with salt and roll in cornflake crumbs. In skillet, sauté chicken in butter until browned. Remove and place in roaster. Add onions to skillet and brown. Turn off heat and add olives, mushrooms, raisins, tomatoes and 1 cup wine. Pour mixture over chicken. Bake uncovered at 350 degrees for 1 hour. Add ½ cup wine and bake 30 minutes longer. Baste while cooking. Serve over rice.

8 servings

CHICKEN PARMESAN

Show ■
Go ■

2 c. seasoned bread
  crumbs
¾ c. grated Parmesan
  cheese
1 tsp. paprika
¼ c. finely chopped
  parsley
1 tsp. oregano
¼ tsp. basil
1-2 tsp. salt
⅛ tsp. pepper
2 (2½-3 lb.) cut-up
  chickens
¾ c. butter or margarine,
  melted

Mix together bread crumbs, cheese, paprika, parsley, oregano, basil, salt and pepper. Dip chicken pieces into melted butter, then roll in bread crumb mixture until well coated. Arrange skin side up in a foil-lined shallow baking pan. Bake at 375 degrees for 1-1½ hours until tender. Do not turn chicken pieces while baking.

8 servings

Additional Parmesan cheese may be sprinkled on top before baking. Any Italian marinara sauce may be poured on top before baking.

CHICKEN AND PASTA

Show ■
Go □

**4 (8 oz.) chicken breasts,
skinned and boned**
¼-½ c. flour
3 eggs, beaten
⅓ c. oil
**½ c. sliced fresh
mushrooms**
½ c. butter
1 tsp. salt
½ tsp. white pepper
garlic powder to taste
**½ lb. fresh or dried
fettuccine noodles,
cooked al dente**
½ c. whipping cream
½ c. milk
**1 c. grated Parmesan
cheese**
2 T. minced parsley

Dip chicken in flour, in eggs and then back in flour. Sauté in oil until golden brown. Dice chicken and set aside. In large skillet, sauté mushrooms in butter. Season with salt, pepper and garlic powder. Add the diced chicken. Mix in noodles, cream, milk and cheese. Serve on warmed plate and sprinkle with additional Parmesan cheese and parsley.

4 servings

Chicken with a kick!

MARINATED CHICKEN

Show ■
Go ■

1 (2½-3 lb.) cut-up chicken
1 clove garlic, crushed
⅔ c. water
¼ c. oil
2 T. lemon juice
2 T. spicy brown mustard
2 tsp. salt
½ tsp. chili powder
½ tsp. sugar (optional)

Place chicken in large bowl. Combine remaining ingredients and pour over chicken. Refrigerate for several hours or overnight, turning chicken two or three times. Drain and reserve marinade.

Preheat broiler for 10 minutes. Put chicken, skin side down, on broiler pan or charcoal grill. Brush with marinade and broil 20 minutes on each side, basting with marinade every 5 minutes.

4-5 servings

CHICKEN IN FILLO WITH MADEIRA SAUCE

Show ■
Go □

3 whole boned chicken breasts, skinned and cut in half
salt and pepper

Mushroom Filling:
1 lb. fresh mushrooms, finely chopped
3 T. onion, chopped
¼ c. unsalted butter
salt
pepper
4-5 tsp. Madeira wine
¼ c. whipping cream

1 pkg. fillo leaves
1 c. unsalted butter, melted

Madeira Sauce:
3 T. butter
1½ T. flour
¾ c. beef stock
1 tsp. Kitchen Bouquet
¼ c. Madeira wine
¼ c. reserved Mushroom Filling

Make a slit, lengthwise in each chicken breast. Place in well-greased baking dish. Season with salt and pepper. Put parchment paper over chicken and tuck into sides of dish. Bake at 450 degrees for 7 minutes. Remove from baking dish and cool.

For filling, over high heat, sauté mushrooms, onion, butter, salt and pepper. Pour in wine and cream. Cook about 5 minutes until mixture coats mushrooms; let cool. Fill each chicken breast with mushroom mixture, reserving ¼ cup for sauce.

Remove 2 sheets of fillo and cover the rest with a damp towel. Brush each sheet with melted butter. Place one chicken breast on the 2 sheets and wrap with dough starting at the narrow edge. Continue to brush dough with butter as you fold. Place seam side down on well greased cookie sheet. Repeat with remaining chicken breasts. Bake at 350 degrees for 20 minutes or until brown. Do not overcook.

For Madeira sauce, melt butter; stir in flour, beef stock and Kitchen Bouquet. Cook 5 minutes. Add Madeira and cook until thickened. Stir in ¼ cup mushroom mixture. Before serving, pour 2 tablespoons hot Madeira sauce over each chicken breast.

6 servings

May be prepared day ahead except for baking.

MEXICAN CHICKEN

Show ■
Go ■

4 whole boned chicken
   breasts, skinned and cut
   in half
8 small chunks Monterey
   Jack cheese
1 egg, beaten
1 c. bread crumbs
2 T. butter or margarine
1 onion, chopped
1 (6 oz.) can pitted ripe
   olives
1 (14 oz.) can mild
   enchilada sauce
2 c. shredded Cheddar
   cheese
crumbled taco chips

Pound chicken breasts thin. Place a chunk of cheese on each breast and shape chicken around it. Dip into egg and then bread crumbs. Melt butter and sauté chicken until lightly browned. Place in 9x13-inch pan, seam side down, and cover with onion, olives and enchilada sauce. Top with cheese and taco chips. Bake at 350 degrees for 1 hour or until bubbly.

6 servings

Chicken can be prepared ahead and baked just before serving.

PURPLE PLUM CHICKEN

Show ■
Go ■

2 (3 lb.) cut-up chickens
garlic and onion salt

Sauce:
1 onion, chopped
3 T. oil
1 (30 oz.) can purple
   plums, drained and
   puréed
1 (6 oz.) can frozen
   lemonade concentrate
⅓ c. chili sauce
¼ c. soy sauce
1 tsp. ginger
2 drops Tabasco
1 tsp. Worcestershire
1½ tsp. dry mustard

Place seasoned chicken, skin side up, on foil-lined greased baking pan or broiler pan with sides and broil until browned. For sauce, sauté onion in oil. Combine remaining ingredients, add to onion and simmer 10 minutes. Pour ½ of sauce over browned chicken. Bake at 350 degrees for 45 minutes, basting frequently with remaining sauce.

6-8 servings

Sauce can also be used for duck and Cornish hens.

TOULOUSE CHICKEN

Show ■
Go ☐

Marinade:
2 c. oil
½ c. dry white wine
½ tsp. salt
¼ tsp. oregano
¼ tsp. garlic powder

4 whole boned chicken breasts, cut in half

Seasoned Butter:
1 c. butter, softened
1 clove garlic, chopped
½ tsp. chopped green onion
¼ tsp. Dijon mustard
dash each of curry powder, thyme, cumin, nutmeg
¾ tsp. chopped almonds
1 T. chopped parsley
½ T. Pernod liqueur
salt and pepper to taste

2 T. oil
¼ tsp. oregano
¼ c. chopped ripe olives
¼ c. pimento-stuffed olives
⅓ c. chopped canned tomatoes

Combine all ingredients for marinade. Place chicken breasts in mixture; cover and refrigerate overnight.

Next day, make seasoned butter by combining listed ingredients. Remove chicken from marinade and brown in 2 tablespoons oil over high heat, skin side up, for 4-5 minutes. Turn and season with ¼ teaspoon oregano. Reduce heat, cover and cook 5-8 minutes longer or until done. Melt seasoned butter mixture in a saucepan, adding olives and tomatoes. Cook on high heat stirring constantly. Place chicken on serving plate and cover with ½ of the sauce. Pass remaining sauce.

8 servings

The chicken you'd cross the road for ...

CHICKEN CACCIATORE

Show ■
Go ■

6 whole chicken breasts
salt
pepper
2 T. olive oil
2 cloves garlic, crushed
8 oz. fresh mushrooms,
  sliced
1 med. onion, chopped
1 med. green pepper,
  chopped
1 (28 oz.) can stewed
  tomatoes
1 (6 oz.) can tomato paste
  (optional)
1 (2¼ oz.) can sliced ripe
  olives
1 (2¼ oz.) can sliced green
  olives
celery seed

Season chicken with salt and pepper. Brown in olive oil with crushed garlic. Add mushrooms, onion, green pepper and sauté until limp. Place mixture in roasting pan and add remaining ingredients. Cook uncovered until sauce reaches spaghetti sauce consistency, approximately 45-55 minutes. Serve over parsley buttered new potatoes, buttered noodles or wild rice.

6 servings

HONEY CURRY CHICKEN

Show ■
Go ■

½ c. butter
½ c. honey
¼ c. prepared mustard
2 tsp. curry powder
pinch of salt
4 whole chicken breasts

In saucepan, melt butter and add honey, mustard, curry powder and salt. Place chicken breasts, skin side up, in 9x13-inch pan. Bake at 350 degrees for 15 minutes. Baste with sauce and continue baking for 1 hour, basting with sauce every 15 minutes until done.

4 servings

TROUT AMANDINE

Show ■
Go ■

2½ lbs. trout fillets,
  skinned
½ c. milk
½ c. flour
salt and pepper, to taste
1 c. butter
6 oz. almonds, roasted
juice of 2 lemons
1 T. chopped parsley

Dip fillets into milk, then dredge in flour, salt and pepper. Melt butter in skillet and fry fillets slowly until brown on both sides. Remove to a warm platter. Sprinkle almonds over fish. Add juice and parsley to skillet and cook a few minutes. Pour sauce over fish and serve.

6 servings

BAKED ITALIAN TROUT

Show ■
Go ■

1 (5 lb.) trout, skinned and
  boned
salt and pepper, to taste
1 egg, slightly beaten
1 c. bread crumbs
grated Parmesan cheese, to
  taste

Season fish with salt and pepper. Dip in egg, then bread crumbs. Sprinkle with Parmesan cheese. Bake at 400 degrees for 10-20 minutes.

5-6 servings

BAKED TROUT IN WINE

Show ■
Go ■

6 rainbow trout, dressed
  and washed
2 T. lemon juice
salt and pepper, to taste
1 c. dry white wine
2 T. chopped parsley
¼ c. sliced green onion
2 T. dry bread crumbs
¼ c. melted butter
fresh dill
6 thin lemon slices

Brush inside of trout with lemon juice and sprinkle with salt and pepper. Arrange trout in shallow baking dish and brush with remaining lemon juice; sprinkle with salt and pepper. Pour wine into baking dish. Cover fish with parsley and onion. Sprinkle with bread crumbs and spoon butter over each fish. Bake uncovered at 400 degrees for 25 minutes or until flaky. Arrange on platter and garnish with dill and lemon slices.

6 servings

ELEGANT CRAB ASPARAGUS

Show ■
Go □

⅓ c. butter
⅓ c. flour
1¼ c. milk
1 tsp. seasoned salt
¼ tsp. pepper
¼ c. grated Parmesan
cheese
2 (6 oz.) pkgs. frozen king
crab, thawed and
drained
2 (15 oz.) cans colossal
white asparagus spears
grated Parmesan cheese
paprika

For sauce, melt butter over low heat and stir in flour until well blended. Add milk and stir constantly. Add salt, pepper and Parmesan cheese and continue cooking until smooth. Set aside. Place crab in greased 2-quart casserole. Sprinkle with salt and pepper if desired. Add ½ cup sauce and mix with crabmeat. Arrange asparagus spears on top and spoon remaining sauce over all. Sprinkle with Parmesan cheese and paprika. Bake at 375 degrees for 30 minutes or until bubbly.

4 servings

Serve with fruit or salad.

SAUCY SHRIMP

Show ■
Go □

1½ lbs. fresh mushrooms,
cleaned
2 T. butter
1 (20 oz.) can artichoke
hearts
1 lb. med. shrimp, cooked

Sauce:
6½ T. butter
4½ T. flour
1½ c. half and half cream
salt and pepper, to taste
½ c. sherry
1 T. Worcestershire

½ c. grated Parmesan
cheese
paprika

Sauté mushrooms in 2 tablespoons butter. Arrange half the artichokes on bottom of 1½-2-quart casserole. Place shrimp and mushrooms over artichokes. Prepare sauce by melting butter in pan and adding flour and cream and stirring constantly. When thickened, season with salt and pepper and add sherry and Worcestershire. Pour sauce in casserole. Arrange remaining artichokes on top of sauce and sprinkle with Parmesan cheese and paprika. Bake at 375 degrees for 20 minutes.

4-6 servings

BUTTERFLIED WOKERY SHRIMP

Show ■
Go ■

2 lbs. raw shrimp, cleaned
  and deveined
2 egg whites
2 T. sherry
2 T. cornstarch
½ c. oil
4 tsp. finely chopped fresh
  ginger
4 tsp. crushed garlic
¼ tsp. chili pepper
4 green onions, chopped
1 tsp. salt
2 T. soy sauce
½ c. ketchup
4 tsp. sugar
4 tsp. cornstarch
½ c. water
2 c. cooked long grain rice

Slit each shrimp part way down the back. Combine egg whites, sherry and 2 tablespoons cornstarch. Marinate shrimp in mixture for 30 minutes. Heat oil in wok and stir fry ginger, garlic, chili pepper and onions 2-3 minutes. Add marinated shrimp and stir-fry 2-4 minutes longer. Add salt, soy sauce, ketchup and sugar and cook a few minutes, being careful not to overcook. Mix 4 teaspoons cornstarch and water; add to shrimp and cook until thickened. Serve with or over white rice.

4-6 servings

For hotter tastes use more chili pepper.

They'd wok a mile for this dish

COLD FILLET OF FISH ROMANOFF

Show ■
Go □

**6 fillets of sole or flounder,
cut in half (about 3 lbs.)**

Court Bouillon:
1 qt. water
1 c. white wine
½ rib celery
1 bay leaf
1 small onion, quartered
½ lemon
6 peppercorns
1 clove garlic, crushed
1 tsp. salt

Sauce:
¾ c. dairy sour cream
¾ c. mayonnaise
¼ tsp. Dijon mustard
1½ tsp. lemon juice
¼ tsp. salt
¼ tsp. pepper
1 clove garlic, crushed
1 shallot, minced
1 (2 oz.) jar red caviar
6 lemon wedges

Roll each fillet and secure with toothpick. Bring court bouillon to a boil in a 10-inch skillet. Reduce heat and simmer for 5 minutes uncovered. Place fish rolls in skillet. Cover and cook 5-6 minutes or until tender. Drain and refrigerate overnight.

Combine sauce ingredients in a small bowl, refrigerate for 6 hours or overnight.

The next day place fish rolls on serving plate. Spoon some of the sauce over fish. Sprinkle each roll with caviar, garnish with lemon wedges. Serve with remaining sauce.

4-6 servings

This must be made the day before serving.

A two day operation

CIOPPINO - SAN FRANCISCO FISH STEW

Show ■
Go ☐

8 green onions, sliced
2 cloves garlic, chopped
1 c. chopped celery
20 fresh mushrooms
⅓ c. olive oil
⅓ c. chopped parsley
1 c. canned tomato purée
1 (8 oz.) can tomato sauce
1 (6 oz.) can tomato paste
2½ c. water
2 c. Sauterne wine
1 tsp. lemon juice
1 bay leaf
1½ tsp. salt
¼ tsp. pepper
½ tsp. allspice
2 lbs. clams, in shell, well
**   scrubbed**
¾ lb. raw shrimp, cleaned
**   and deveined**
1 lb. red snapper or halibut
**   fillet, cut into 1-inch**
**   chunks**
¾-1 lb. crabmeat

In a 6-8 quart pot, sauté onions, garlic, celery and mushrooms in oil. Add all remaining ingredients except fish and seafood. Bring to a boil; reduce heat and simmer for 2 hours. Add clams and cook until shells open. Add shrimp and snapper and cook until fish flakes easily. Add crabmeat and heat thoroughly.

Types and amounts of seafood may vary. Great served with thick slices of garlic bread.

6 servings

JAMBALAYA

Show ■
Go ■

1 lb. smoked salami or
   beer sticks, cubed
½ c. oil
2 med. onions, chopped
8 green onions, chopped
1 lb. fresh mushrooms,
   sliced
1 lg. green pepper,
   chopped
½ c. diced celery
¼ tsp. thyme
2 bay leaves
4 cloves garlic
½ tsp. salt
dash red cayenne pepper
2 lbs. raw shrimp, peeled
   and deveined
2 (16 oz.) cans tomatoes,
   including liquid
1 (6 oz.) can tomato paste
½ lemon, quartered
3 cups cooked long grain
   rice

In a 4-quart Dutch oven, brown salami in hot oil. Add onions, mushrooms, green pepper, celery, thyme, bay leaves, garlic, salt and red pepper. Cook 3 minutes. Add shrimp, tomatoes, tomato paste and lemon. Simmer slowly, uncovered, tossing ingredients often until shrimp is pink. Remove bay leaves and lemon. Add rice and toss all together; serve.

8-10 servings

a New Orleans specialty

SALMON MOUSSE

Show ■
Go ☐

1 (8 oz.) pkg. cream cheese
1 (10¾ oz.) can tomato
  soup
2½ T. unflavored gelatin
½ c. cold water
1 c. mayonnaise
1 (16 oz.) can red salmon,
  drained and flaked
½ c. finely chopped celery
½ c. finely chopped green
  pepper

Sauce:
1 c. dairy sour cream
1-2 T. dry onion soup mix
½ c. diced cucumber

Heat cream cheese and soup until creamy. Beat with rotary beater. Dissolve gelatin in water and mix into soup. When cool, add mayonnaise. Fold in salmon, celery, green pepper and pour into oiled 2½-quart dish or fish mold. Refrigerate overnight.

For sauce, combine sour cream, onion soup mix and cucumber. Serve in separate bowl.

16 servings

Great luncheon dish or appetizer with toast rounds. May substitute 3 (7 oz.) cans of water packed tuna for salmon.

SALMON PATTIES

Show ☐
Go ■

1 (16 oz.) can red salmon,
  drained and flaked
4 eggs, slightly beaten
salt and pepper to taste
1 c. dairy sour cream
1 c. crushed corn flakes
2 T. minced green onions
oil for frying

Mix all ingredients except oil in bowl. Place in refrigerator for 15 minutes. Shape mixture into patties. Fry until brown on one side. Turn and brown other side.

12 patties

May top with fried mushrooms and onions or Mushroom Sauce (see index). Also good cold.

ROSEMARY VEAL CHOPS

Show ■
Go ■

4 (½-in. thick) veal chops, boned
2 eggs, slightly beaten
1-2 tsp. rosemary
salt and pepper to taste
1 c. bread crumbs
3 T. olive oil
2 T. butter
4 cloves garlic, halved

Pound veal between two pieces of waxed paper. Dip veal into beaten eggs. Sprinkle with rosemary, salt and pepper and dip into bread crumbs. In large skillet, heat oil, butter and garlic. Add veal and cook on medium to high heat about 15 minutes or until golden brown. Discard garlic and place chops on a serving dish.

4 servings

MINNESOTA VEAL STEW

Show ■
Go ■

4 lbs. veal shoulder or breast, boned and cubed
salt and pepper
¼ c. oil
2 c. finely chopped onions
1 T. chopped garlic
1 tsp. saffron (optional)
¼ c. flour
¼ c. dry white wine
1 (28 oz.) can peeled tomatoes, chopped
1 c. chicken broth
2 tsp. rosemary
buttered noodles or rice

Sprinkle veal with salt and pepper. Heat oil in a large Dutch oven. Add veal, cook for 20 minutes, stirring frequently until liquid evaporates and meat is browned. Add onions, garlic and saffron. Cook, stirring occasionally, about 5 minutes. Sprinkle with flour, stir to coat meat evenly. Add wine, tomatoes, broth, rosemary and salt and pepper to taste. Cover and bake at 375 degrees for 1 hour. Serve over noodles or rice.

8 servings

a real Minnesota rouser

89

VEAL DAUBE

Show ☐
Go ■

1 (4-5 lb.) veal shoulder
  roast
1 clove garlic
¼ c. flour
1 tsp. salt
⅛ tsp. pepper
¼ tsp. allspice
½ tsp. each thyme and
  sage
2 bay leaves, crushed
oil for browning
1 med. onion, minced
4 carrots, sliced
2 ribs celery, including
  leaves, diced
1 c. boiling water

Rub roast all over with cut garlic and dredge roast in mixture of flour and spices. In a heavy pan, brown in oil until crust forms. Remove meat. Brown vegetables in same pan and return meat. Add boiling water, cover and cook slowly over low heat 2-2½ hours or until tender.

8 servings

BLUE HORSE VEAL PICCATA

Show ■
Go ■

12 (3 oz.) pieces veal sliced
  for scaloppine
salt
freshly ground pepper
1 c. flour
½ c. olive oil
¼ c. Shallot Butter (see
  index)
⅓ c. dry white wine
juice of 1 lemon
8 lemon slices
2 T. chopped parsley

Pound veal slices until thin. Sprinkle with salt and pepper and dredge lightly in flour. Heat olive oil in a large skillet and sauté veal on both sides until lightly browned. Transfer to a hot platter. Pour off oil from pan and add Shallot Butter, wine and lemon juice. When butter has melted and the liquid begins to boil, return veal to pan. Turn pieces frequently, allowing the sauce to reduce to a glazed consistency. Remove veal, place on hot platter and top with reduced sauce. Garnish with lemon slices and fresh chopped parsley.

6 servings

VEAL SUPREME

Show ■
Go □

1½ lbs. veal cutlets,
   pounded slightly
½ c. flour
garlic powder, to taste
pinch of salt
2 eggs, beaten
2 T. milk
¾ c. bread crumbs
¼ c. oil
2 (8 oz.) jars marinara sauce

Cheese Topping:
3 T. butter
3 T. flour
½ tsp. salt
1½ c. milk
4 oz. Gruyere cheese, cut
   in chunks
¼ c. grated Parmesan
   cheese

Parmesan cheese, paprika
   for garnish

Dredge veal in mixture of flour, garlic powder and salt. Combine eggs and 2 tablespoons milk and dip veal first in eggs and then in bread crumbs. Brown in oil on both sides. Pour marinara sauce into a large pan and place veal in sauce.

For topping, melt butter in saucepan, add flour, salt, 1½ cups milk, Gruyere and Parmesan cheeses. Stir well to blend and pour sauce over veal. Garnish with more Parmesan cheese and paprika. Bake uncovered at 350 degrees for 45 minutes or until brown.

6 servings

LEMON VEAL

Show ■
Go ■

2 lbs. veal sliced for
   scaloppine
2 eggs, beaten
½ c. flour
½ c. butter
1 lemon

Dip veal in eggs and then in flour. Sauté in butter in large skillet, turning until brown on both sides. Remove and place on serving platter. Squeeze lemon juice into hot pan, stir and pour over veal.

4 servings

Serve with buttered noodles and fried zucchini.

VEAL MARSALA

Show ■
Go ■

2 lbs. veal sliced for
    scaloppine
1 c. flour
¼ c. butter
garlic salt
salt
pepper
2 (10 oz.) cans beef
    consommé
¼ c. Marsala wine
1 lg. onion, chopped
1 med. green pepper,
    chopped
½ lb. fresh mushrooms,
    sliced
2 (8 oz.) pkgs. noodles,
    cooked al dente

Dredge veal in flour. Melt butter in a large skillet and brown veal lightly on both sides. Season with salts and pepper. Add consommé and simmer uncovered 10-15 minutes. Add wine and simmer uncovered 2-3 minutes. Place veal in a 9x13-inch baking dish or casserole and cover with pan juices. Sauté onion, pepper and mushrooms and spread over veal. Bake at 325 degrees, uncovered, for 20 minutes. Serve over noodles.

6-8 servings

VEAL, PEPPERS AND ONIONS

Show ■
Go ■

2½ lbs. veal sliced for
    scaloppine
3 eggs, beaten
1 c. bread crumbs
½ c. olive oil
1 c. sherry
1 c. water
6 beef bouillon cubes
½ lb. fresh mushrooms,
    sliced
3 cloves garlic, peeled
2 (7 oz.) jars Progresso
    sweet peppers and
    onions

Dip veal in eggs and then into bread crumbs. Sauté in oil until browned on both sides. In a saucepan, bring sherry, water and bouillon cubes to a boil. Add mushrooms, garlic, peppers and onions. Place veal in a 9x13-inch baking dish. Pour sherry mixture over the veal; remove garlic cloves. Bake at 350 degrees for 30 minutes.

8 servings

VEAL PARMIGIANI

Show ■
Go ☐

Sauce:
5 T. oil
1 lg. onion, chopped
2 cloves garlic, mashed
2 (16 oz.) cans tomato
    sauce
½ c. water
1 tsp. basil
1 tsp. oregano
½ tsp. seasoned salt
¼ tsp. sugar
¼ tsp. pepper
2 T. chopped parsley

1 lb. veal, sliced for
    scaloppine
½ c. grated Parmesan
    cheese
½ c. fine dry bread crumbs
2 eggs, slightly beaten
¼ c. oil
1 (16 oz.) pkg. Mozzarella
    cheese, sliced
3 T. grated Parmesan
    cheese
2 (8 oz.) pkgs. noodles,
    cooked al dente

To make sauce, heat oil in saucepan. Sauté onion and garlic until golden. Stir in tomato sauce, water, basil, oregano, salt, sugar, pepper and parsley. Cover and simmer 10 minutes.

For veal, combine ½ cup Parmesan cheese and ½ cup bread crumbs. Dip veal slices into beaten egg, then in cheese and bread crumb mixture. Heat 2 tablespoons oil in skillet and sauté veal until golden brown, turning only once. Repeat with remaining veal and oil.

Pour half the tomato mixture into a 9x13-inch baking dish. Lay Mozzarella cheese over sauce, then veal. Continue to layer cheese and veal ending with cheese. Pour remaining sauce over top. Sprinkle with 3 tablespoons Parmesan cheese. Bake at 350 degrees for 25 minutes or until sauce is bubbly and cheese melts. Serve with noodles.

4-6 servings

reVeal your cooking talents

DAIRY LASAGNE

Show ■
Go □

Sauce:
1 c. chopped onions
1 clove garlic, crushed
¼ c. oil
2 (19 oz.) cans tomatoes
1 (6 oz.) can tomato paste
1 (8 oz.) can tomato sauce
2 T. chopped parsley
1 T. salt
1 T. sugar
1 T. oregano
1½ tsp. basil
1 T. pepper

Noodles:
1 (8 oz.) pkg. lasagne
    noodles, cooked

Filling:
2 lbs. dry cottage cheese
12 oz. shredded Mozzarella
    cheese
½ c. grated Parmesan
    cheese
2 eggs
1 T. chopped parsley
1 tsp. salt
¼ tsp. pepper

Topping:
grated Parmesan cheese, to
    taste
4 oz. shredded Mozzarella
    cheese

For sauce, sauté onions and garlic in oil. Add remaining sauce ingredients and simmer 1 hour. Combine filling ingredients. Pour layer of sauce into greased 10x14-inch pan to cover bottom. Add layer of cooked noodles and layer of filling, repeating layers of sauce, noodles and filling until all are used. Top with Parmesan and Mozzarella cheeses. Bake at 375 degrees for 30 minutes.

12-16 servings

Healthy, "cheesey", & wise

LINGUINE WITH CLAM SAUCE

Show ■
Go ■

3 cloves garlic, crushed
¾ c. light olive oil
1 c. butter
2 doz. cherrystone clams,
   shucked or 2 (7½ oz.)
   cans minced clams
½ c. finely chopped
   parsley
1 tsp. basil
½ tsp. oregano
crushed red pepper
freshly ground black
   pepper
1½ lbs. linguine, cooked al
   dente
grated Parmesan cheese

Sauté garlic in oil and butter for 5 minutes. Add clams, parsley, basil, oregano and peppers. Simmer 20 minutres, stirring occasionally. Serve over linguine. Top with Parmesan cheese.

4-6 servings

CHILES RELLENOS PIE

Show ■
Go ■

2 (4 oz.) cans mild green
   chiles, seeds removed
1 lb. shredded Cheddar
   cheese
1 lb. shredded Monterey
   Jack cheese
¼ c. flour
1 (13 oz.) can evaporated
   milk
4 eggs
1 (8 oz.) can tomato sauce

Line a 9x13-inch baking dish with chiles. Sprinkle with ⅓ of each cheese. Add another layer of chiles and ⅓ more cheese. Mix flour, milk and eggs in food processor or blender. Pour over cheeses. Sprinkle on remaining cheese. Bake at 375 degrees for 30 minutes. Pour tomato sauce on top and bake 15 minutes longer. Can be frozen and reheated.

8-10 servings

MANICOTTI

Show ■
Go □

Sauce:
¼ c. olive oil
1 clove garlic, chopped
1 (28 oz.) can tomatoes
    with liquid
2 (6 oz.) cans tomato paste
2 T. chopped parsley
1 tsp. salt
1 T. sugar
½ c. chopped onion
¼ tsp. oregano
¼ tsp. basil
¼ tsp. pepper
2 T. butter

Filling:
¾ c. Ricotta cheese
12 oz. Mozzarella cheese,
    diced
½ c. grated Parmesan
    cheese
3 eggs
1 tsp. salt
¼ tsp. pepper
½ c. chopped parsley
½ c. grated Parmesan
    cheese, for topping

1 (8 oz.) pkg. manicotti
    noodles, cooked,
    drained and cooled

Combine all ingredients for sauce and heat to boiling. Reduce heat and simmer one hour. In a large bowl, combine all filling ingredients except ½ cup Parmesan cheese. Stuff manicotti with filling and place in greased 9x13-inch baking dish. Pour sauce over noodles and sprinkle with remaining Parmesan cheese. Bake at 350 degrees for 45 minutes.

6 servings

Sauce may be made ahead of time and refrigerated.

ITALIAN MAIN DISH PIE

Show ■
Go ■

1 (9-in.) unbaked frozen pie crust (or own recipe)
6 eggs
¼ c. milk
1 (7 oz.) can tuna, drained and flaked or 1 c. flaked cooked fish
8 oz. shredded Mozzarella cheese
¼ tsp. salt
¼ tsp. ground pepper
½ tsp. basil
½ tsp. oregano

Line a quiche pan with pastry, if not using prepared pie shell. Beat eggs and milk until blended. Add remaining ingredients and stir well. Spoon into crust. Bake at 425 degrees for 35-40 minutes or until brown. Cut into wedges and serve hot.

6 servings

SPINACH QUICHE

Show ■
Go ■

1 (10 oz.) pkg. frozen chopped spinach, cooked and drained
8 oz. shredded Cheddar cheese
4 oz. shredded Mozzarella cheese
3 eggs, beaten
2 c. skim milk
1 (2.8 oz.) can French fried onion rings
¼ tsp. salt
¼ tsp. pepper
3-4 drops Tabasco

Mix cooled spinach with cheeses, eggs, milk, onions and spices. Pour into 9-inch quiche pan and bake at 350 degrees for 40 minutes.

6-8 servings

HE-MAN quiche

HOOTENANNY PANCAKE

Show ☐
Go ■

½ c. butter
6 eggs
1 c. milk
1 c. flour
½ tsp. salt
maple syrup or jam

Melt butter in a 9x13-inch glass baking dish. Beat eggs, milk, flour and salt together. Add to pan without stirring. Bake at 400 degrees for 25-30 minutes. Cut in large squares and serve immediately. Top with maple syrup or jam.

4-6 servings

Also good with sliced apples, sautéed in butter and sprinkled with cinnamon-sugar mixture.

BRUNCH EGG CASSEROLE

Show ■
Go ■

2 c. seasoned croutons
1½-2 c. shredded Cheddar cheese
4 eggs, slightly beaten
2 c. milk
½ tsp. salt
½ tsp. dry mustard
⅛ tsp. onion powder
dash of pepper

Combine croutons and cheese in a greased 2-quart baking dish. Mix remaining ingredients in a large bowl with electric mixer until well blended. Pour egg mixture over croutons. Bake at 325 degrees for 55-60 minutes or until golden brown.

6 servings

Serve a bunch for brunch!

Vegetables and Side Dishes

ISRAELI SKILLET EGGPLANT

Show ■
Go ■

1 med. eggplant, skin on
1 med. onion, peeled
1 med. green pepper
2 tomatoes, peeled
¼ c. oil
1 clove garlic, chopped
2 tsp. salt
½ tsp. pepper

Cut eggplant, onion, green pepper and tomatoes into chunks. Heat oil, garlic, salt and pepper in skillet. Add vegetables except tomatoes, cover and simmer, stirring occasionally about 12-14 minutes or until tender. Add tomatoes last 5 minutes. Serve immediately or place in casserole and keep warm in 300 degree oven.

4-6 servings

May top with Parmesan or shredded Mozzarella cheese before baking.

MOM'S LIMA BEANS

Show ■
Go ■

6 (15½ oz.) cans butter
  beans
¾ c. brown sugar, packed
¼ c. tomato soup,
  undiluted
1 c. ketchup
½ c. whipping cream
1 tsp. dry mustard
6 T. butter, softened
salt and pepper to taste

Drain beans well and place in 3-quart casserole; mix in remaining ingredients. Bake uncovered at 375 degrees for 45-50 minutes.

18-20 servings

Mama knows best!

SPINACH SQUARES

Show ■
Go ■

**2 (10 oz.) pkgs. frozen
spinach, cooked and
drained
¼ c. flour
1 tsp. salt
¼ tsp. pepper
6 eggs, well beaten
1 (24 oz.) carton large curd
cottage cheese
12 oz. shredded sharp
Cheddar cheese
¼ c. bread crumbs**

Mix spinach well with flour, salt and pepper; add eggs, cottage cheese and Cheddar cheese. Place in greased 9x13-inch glass baking dish; top with bread crumbs. Bake at 350 degrees for 45 minutes. Remove from oven and let stand a few minutes before cutting.

10-12 servings

May be frozen after baking; defrost and heat.

SPINACH ROLL WITH MUSHROOM SAUCE

Show ■
Go ■

**2 (10 oz.) pkgs. frozen
chopped spinach,
thawed and drained
2 eggs
1 envelope dry onion soup
mix
⅔ c. Ricotta cheese
Mushroom Sauce, (see
index)**

Blend spinach, eggs and onion soup mix in a blender or food processor. Spread on a greased 10½x15½-inch jelly roll pan or cookie sheet. Square edges to form a 9x13-inch rectangle. Bake at 350 degrees for 20 minutes. Gently release from pan. Whip Ricotta cheese and spread over baked spinach. Starting at narrow end, roll up like a jelly roll. Heat at 350 degrees for 10 minutes or until hot. Serve with Mushroom Sauce.

6 servings

SIMPLE SPINACH SOUFFLE

Show ■
Go ■

½ onion, chopped
1 T. butter
1¼ T. flour
1 (10 oz.) pkg. frozen
   chopped spinach,
   cooked and drained
1 c. cottage cheese
3 eggs, beaten well
salt
pepper
grated Parmesan cheese
nutmeg

Sauté onion in melted butter, add flour and spinach. Mix in cottage cheese, eggs, salt and pepper. Place in buttered 1½-quart casserole. Sprinkle with Parmesan cheese and nutmeg and set in pan of hot water. Bake uncovered at 350 degrees for 1 hour.

6-8 servings

LAYERED VEGETABLE SOUFFLE

Show ■
Go ■

2-3 (12 oz.) pkgs. frozen
   Stouffer's Spinach
   Soufflé
2-3 (12 oz.) pkgs. frozen
   Stouffer's Corn Soufflé
1 (16 oz.) pkg. frozen
   sliced or baby carrots
2 T. butter (optional)
2 T. brown sugar (optional)

Place frozen layer of each vegetable in 9x13-inch baking dish. Dot with butter and sprinkle with brown sugar, if desired. Bake uncovered at 350 degrees for 1 hour or until puffy. Serve immediately.

10-12 servings

May omit brown sugar and sprinkle with Parmesan cheese.

So easy it's embarrassing!

CARROT BROCCOLI SUPREME

Show ■
Go ■

1½ c. sliced carrots
1 med. onion, sliced
1 (10 oz.) pkg. frozen
  broccoli
3 T. butter
3 T. flour
1½ c. milk
1 c. shredded sharp
  Cheddar cheese
¼ tsp. salt
dash each pepper, dry
  mustard, cayenne and
  Worcestershire
1 (2.8 oz.) can French fried
  onion rings

Cook carrots and onion until tender. Set aside. Cook and drain broccoli. In a separate saucepan melt butter; remove from heat and add flour gradually. Return to heat, add milk, stirring constantly until mixture thickens. Add cheese and spices. Grease an 8x8-inch pan and layer broccoli, carrots, onion and sauce, ending with sauce. Bake at 350 degrees for 45 minutes. Sprinkle onion rings on top and bake for 15 minutes more.

6 servings

Recipe may be doubled in a 9x13-inch pan.

ZUCCHINI SOUFFLE

Show ■
Go ■

½ tsp. salt
6 c. grated zucchini
1 med. onion, sliced
2 T. butter
4 eggs
¼ c. milk
¾ c. bread crumbs
½ tsp. basil
½ tsp. oregano
1 c. shredded Mozzarella
  cheese

Sprinkle salt over zucchini in large bowl and let rest for 10 minutes. Sauté onion in butter. Squeeze excess water from zucchini and add onion. Beat eggs and milk slightly and mix with zucchini. Add bread crumbs and spices. Pour into a greased 2-quart soufflé dish and bake at 400 degrees for 30 minutes. Cover with cheese and bake another 10 minutes or until knife inserted in center comes out clean. Serve immediately.

8-10 servings

BAKED ZUCCHINI

Show ■
Go ■

4 c. chopped zucchini
1 c. Bisquick
4 eggs, slightly beaten
½ c. oil
1 onion, finely chopped
1 c. shredded Monterey
    Jack cheese
1 tsp. cinnamon
1 T. chopped parsley
salt
pepper

Mix all ingredients together in one bowl. Put in 3-quart buttered casserole. Bake at 350 degrees for 30 minutes. Let stand 10 minutes.

6-8 servings

ZUCCHINI CUSTARD

Show ■
Go ■

4 lg. zucchini, sliced
1 egg
½ c. dairy sour cream
¾ tsp. Jane's Krazy Mixed-
    up Salt
¼ tsp. pepper
1 c. freshly grated
    Parmesan cheese
2 T. butter

Cook zucchini, covered, in salted, boiling water until tender. Drain well. Place in shallow baking dish or quiche pan. Mix egg, sour cream, salt, pepper and ½ cup cheese together by hand. Pour over zucchini. Dot with butter and remaining cheese. Bake at 400 degrees for 15 minutes.

6 servings

When doubling recipe, double baking time.

Zucchini's last stand!

ROADSIDE POTATOES

Show ■
Go ■

1 (32 oz.) pkg. frozen hash
  brown potatoes, thawed
½ c. butter, melted
1 c. shredded Cheddar
  cheese
1 c. grated Parmesan
  cheese
¾ c. half and half cream
1 med. onion, grated
salt
pepper
paprika
6 T. butter

Combine potatoes, melted butter, cheeses, cream, onion, salt and pepper. Spread mixture in 9x13-inch well greased baking dish. Sprinkle with paprika; dot with butter. Bake at 350 degrees for 1½ hours.

8-10 servings

The mixture can also be baked in greased muffin tins for only 45-50 minutes. Let stand one minute before removing from pan.

30 muffins

AU GRATIN POTATOES

Show ■
Go ■

1 sm. onion, finely
  chopped
1 (32 oz.) pkg. frozen hash
  brown potatoes, thawed
1 (10½ oz.) can cream of
  mushroom soup
12 oz. dairy sour cream
12 oz. shredded Cheddar
  cheese
¾ c. corn flakes
¼ c. butter, melted

Mix onion, potatoes, soup, sour cream and cheese together and place in a greased 9x13-inch baking dish. Sprinkle with corn flakes and melted butter. Bake at 350 degrees for 1¼ hours.

8-10 servings

Enjoy! Enjoy!

PARMESAN POTATOES

Show ■
Go ■

½ c. unsalted butter
Parmesan cheese
5 med. potatoes, scrubbed
garlic salt
seasoned salt
paprika

Melt butter in foil-lined 10½x15½-inch jelly roll pan. Sprinkle a thin layer of Parmesan cheese over butter. Cut potatoes in half lengthwise and place in pan, skin side up. Season with salts and paprika. Spoon some of the butter over top and add more seasoning. Bake uncovered at 350 degrees for 1-1½ hours or until crispy.

5-10 servings

DOUBLE CREAM MASHED POTATOES

Show ■
Go ■

9 lg. potatoes, peeled and
  boiled
2 (3 oz.) pkgs. cream
  cheese, softened
2 tsp. onion salt
1 tsp. salt
¼ tsp. pepper
2 T. butter or margarine
1 c. dairy sour cream
1 T. butter
paprika

Mash potatoes and beat together with cream cheese, salts, pepper, 2 tablespoons butter and sour cream. Spread in a greased 9x13-inch pan. Cover and refrigerate several hours or overnight.
Dot with remaining butter and sprinkle with paprika. Bake at 350 degrees for 30 minutes.

8-10 servings

Throw calories to the wind!

ONION CASSEROLE

Show ■
Go ☐

¼ c. unsalted butter
7-8 lg. onions, cut into
 chunks
½ c. uncooked rice
1 tsp. salt
5 c. water
1 c. grated Jarlsberg or
 Swiss cheese
⅔ c. half and half cream
salt

In large skillet, melt butter over medium heat and sauté onions until transparent. Remove from heat. Cook rice in boiling, salted water 5 minutes. Drain well. Add rice, cheese and cream to onions and mix well. Salt to taste. Place mixture in greased 2-quart shallow casserole. Bake at 325 degrees for 1 hour. May be served hot or cold.

6-8 servings

VEGETABLE KASHA CASSEROLE

Show ■
Go ■

1½ c. kasha
3 eggs
1 envelope dry onion soup
 mix
3 c. water
1 (16 oz.) pkg. frozen or
 fresh mixed vegetables
1 T. butter
salt
pepper
1 (10½ oz.) can cream of
 mushroom soup

Mix kasha and 1 egg in pan and heat for 1 or 2 minutes, stirring constantly. Remove from heat. Boil onion soup in water for 5-10 minutes. Add soup to kasha and cover pan tightly for 8-10 minutes until kasha is tender. Cook vegetables 5-8 minutes until they are crisp and tender. Butter and season to taste. Beat remaining eggs and add to vegetables. Butter a 2-quart casserole and put in ½ of the kasha mixture. Put vegetables on top. Add mushroom soup to remaining kasha and spread on top of casserole. Bake at 350 degrees for 1 hour.

8-10 servings

MUSHROOM STRUDEL

Show ■
Go □

2 lbs. fresh mushrooms, minced
1 c. minced onion
8 shallots, minced
4-6 T. butter
2 T. oil
1 c. dairy sour cream
¼ c. minced fresh dill weed
salt and pepper
28 fillo strudel leaves
¾ to 1 c. butter, melted

Place mushrooms in towel, a handful at a time and squeeze out moisture. Sauté onion and shallots in skillet in butter and oil until all moisture is evaporated. Add sour cream, dill weed, salt and pepper. (If filling seems too thin, add a little flour to thicken.)

For each roll, place 1 fillo leaf on waxed paper. Brush well with butter. Repeat until 7 leaves are stacked and buttered. Keep remaining leaves covered with damp towel.

Spread a 1-inch wide strip of mushroom filling on long side of buttered fillo leaf. Fold in sides and roll up. Transfer roll to greased cookie sheet and place seam side down. Brush with melted butter. Repeat with other 3 rolls.

Bake at 350 degrees for 45 minutes or until crisp and golden. Cool 5 minutes. Cut diagonal slices 1 inch thick and serve warm.

36 slices

To freeze: Place unbaked on cookie sheet; when frozen wrap individually and return to freezer. Also makes a nice appetizer.

Cave in on this one!

MUSHROOM RICE MOLD

Show ■
Go ■

1 c. uncooked rice
8 oz. fresh mushrooms,
    sliced
1-2 cloves garlic, crushed
2-3 onions, finely chopped
¼ c. butter
salt
pepper

Cook rice as directed on package. Sauté mushrooms, garlic and onions in butter until soft but not overcooked. Add vegetables to rice and season to taste. Mix well and place in 6½-cup ring mold. Bake at 350 degrees for 30 minutes. Invert on serving plate. Fill center with your favorite cooked vegetable.

6-8 servings

BROWN RICE STRUDEL

Show ■
Go □

1½ c. uncooked brown rice
3 c. boiling water
1 c. chopped onions
1 c. chopped fresh
    mushrooms
2 T. butter
2 T. sesame seeds
3 c. shredded Cheddar
    cheese
1 tsp. salt
½ tsp. white pepper
½ c. butter, softened
10 fillo strudel leaves
melted butter
sesame seeds

Cook rice in water for 1 hour. Let cool. Sauté onions and mushrooms in butter until tender. Add sesame seeds and cook another minute. Add to rice and shredded cheese, salt and pepper. Cool mixture thoroughly.

Butter and stack 5 fillo leaves; place ½ of filling mixture on narrow end of fillo leaves and roll up. Slash top in 5 places, brush with melted butter and sprinkle with sesame seeds. Repeat for second roll. Cover with plastic wrap and refrigerate until butter is firm or until ready to use. Rolls may be frozen or refrigerated until the next day.

Place on greased cookie sheet. Bake at 350 degrees for 30 minutes. (If frozen, partially thaw before baking.) Cut each roll in 6 pieces for side dish or larger for main course.

12 servings

ALMOND FRIED RICE

Show ■
Go ■

1½ c. uncooked rice
¼ c. salad oil
⅔ c. chopped green onion
⅔ c. chopped green
  pepper
1 clove garlic, finely
  chopped
1 tsp. salt
¼ tsp. black pepper
½ c. soy sauce
1 c. sliced almonds

Cook rice as directed on package. In large skillet, heat oil; sauté onion, green pepper, garlic, salt and pepper until lightly browned. Add rice, soy sauce and almonds. Sauté 10 minutes, stirring lightly as it cooks.

6 servings

GREEN RICE

Show ■
Go ■

1 c. plus 1 T. uncooked
  rice
2-3 T. chicken broth
½ c. butter
1 med. green pepper
4 green onions
2½ T. chopped fresh
  parsley
1 tsp. salt

Cook rice as directed on package, adding chicken broth to water. Cool and place in large mixing bowl. Melt butter; add to rice and set aside. In blender or food processor, chop green pepper and onions, add to rice with parsley and salt. Pour into a lightly greased 4½-cup mold. Cover and bake at 350 degrees for 1 hour.

8-10 servings

This is great with pepper steak or any chicken dish.

Holiday on rice!

FILLO DE ESPINARDS

Show ■
Go □

2 lbs. fresh spinach,
   washed or 2 (10 oz.)
   pkgs. frozen spinach
8 oz. shredded Mozzarella
   cheese
1 c. freshly grated
   Parmesan cheese
¼ c. cold butter, cut into
   small pieces
salt and pepper to taste
cinnamon, 3 good shakes
½ c. finely chopped green
   onions
1 c. unsalted butter,
   melted
1 pkg. fillo strudel leaves
bread crumbs
finely chopped parsley

If using fresh spinach, place in boiling water for a few minutes. Drain well. Remove stems and chop leaves finely. If using frozen spinach, thaw and drain completely. Add cheeses, ¼ cup butter, salt, pepper, cinnamon and onions. Mix thoroughly.

Brush with butter and stack 6 fillo leaves, sprinkling bread crumbs on each leaf. Place ⅓ of filling mixture on long ends of leaves. Roll up, jelly roll fashion, folding in ends. Place on greased cookie sheet, seam side down. Brush with melted butter and sprinkle with parsley. Repeat for 2 more rolls.

Bake at 400 degrees for 15 minutes. Remove from oven, cut with serrated knife into serving portions. Return to oven and bake 10 minutes or until golden brown.

8-10 servings

May be assembled the day before and baked just before serving. To freeze: Prepare to baking stage and wrap tightly. Thaw before baking.

STRAW AND HAY

Show ■
Go □

2 T. butter
¾ lb. fresh mushrooms, thickly sliced
salt and pepper
½ c. whipping cream or half and half
½-¾ lb. egg fettuccine
½-¾ lb. spinach fettuccine
2 T. Pesto Sauce (see index)
2 T. butter
⅓ c. chicken stock, heated
1 c. whipping cream or half and half
freshly grated Parmesan cheese

In large skillet melt 2 tablespoons butter and sauté mushrooms until tender. Season to taste with salt and pepper. Add ½ cup cream and cook until cream thickens slightly. Set aside. Cook both fettuccines al dente. Drain and return to large pot. Stir in Pesto Sauce and 2 tablespoons butter and mix until melted. Add chicken stock and toss to moisten. Add 1 cup cream and cook gently until sauce thickens slightly. Add mushroom-cream mixture. Taste and correct seasoning. Serve freshly grated Parmesan cheese on the side.

12 servings

NOODLES FLORENTINE

Show ■
Go ■

1 (10 oz.) pkg. broad noodles
1 (10½ oz.) can cream of mushroom soup
½ soup can milk
¾ c. shredded Cheddar cheese
2 (12 oz.) pkgs. frozen spinach soufflé, thawed
½ c. butter
bread crumbs
¼ c. shredded Cheddar cheese

Cook and drain noodles. Mix mushroom soup, milk and ¾ cup cheese and add to noodles. Fold in spinach soufflé and pour into 1½-quart greased casserole. Melt butter and combine with bread crumbs. Mix ¼ cup cheese with buttered bread crumbs and sprinkle over top of casserole. Bake at 350 degrees for 1 hour.

6 servings

BLUE HORSE FETTUCCINE ALFREDO

Show ■
Go ■

1 lb. fettuccine
2 T. butter
1 c. whipping cream
2 egg yolks
pinch of salt
freshly ground pepper to
  taste
¼ c. grated Parmesan
  cheese

Cook fettuccine al dente in rapidly boiling salted water. Drain well and toss in pan over low heat until quite dry. Add butter, cream, egg yolks, salt and pepper and mix well. When hot, add Parmesan cheese and continue tossing lightly until well blended. Place on individual plates, sprinkle lightly with more Parmesan cheese and serve immediately.

4-6 servings

SPINACH FETTUCCINE

Show ■
Go ■

1 lb. fresh spinach or 1 (10
  oz.) pkg. frozen spinach
2 cloves garlic, chopped
2 T. chopped pignoli (pine
  nuts)
½ c. chopped walnuts
½ c. Ricotta cheese
½ c. grated Parmesan
  cheese
¼ tsp. ginger
¼ tsp. nutmeg
1 lb. fettuccine
½ c. butter
1 c. whipping cream
nutmeg and walnut pieces
  for garnish

Cook spinach and drain well. In a large bowl, mix garlic and nuts with cheeses and spices. Cook fettuccine al dente. Drain and return to saucepan. Add butter and cream and cook over high heat. Stir in cheese mixture and toss well. Serve hot. Garnish with nutmeg and walnut pieces.

4-6 servings

PASTA PRIMAVERA

Show ■
Go ☐

1 lb. fresh broccoli
1 med. zucchini
½ lb. fresh asparagus
1 lb. linguine noodles
1 clove garlic, finely
chopped
1 pt. cherry tomatoes,
halved
¼ c. olive oil
¼ c. chopped fresh basil
½ lb. fresh mushrooms,
sliced
¼ c. chopped fresh parsley
1½ tsp. salt
¼ tsp. pepper
¼ tsp. crushed red pepper
¼ c. butter
¾ c. whipping cream
⅔ c. grated Parmesan
cheese

Wash and trim broccoli, zucchini and asparagus. Cut into bite-size pieces. Cook in salted boiling water. Cook and drain linguine, set both aside in large bowls. Sauté garlic and tomatoes in oil for 2 minutes. Stir in basil and mushrooms. Cook 3 minutes. Add parsley, salt and peppers. Cook 1 more minute. Add mixture to vegetables. Melt butter in separate pan. Add cream and cheese. Cook over low heat, stirring constantly until smooth. Add cooked linguine. Toss to coat. Stir in vegetables and heat gently until hot.

8-10 servings

Do not overcook vegetables.

Pasta to lasta lifetime

INDIVIDUAL NOODLE KUGELS

Show ■
Go □

1 (8 oz.) pkg. med. noodles
⅓ c. butter, softened
2 eggs
1 T. sugar
3 T. brown sugar
1 tsp. cinnamon
¼ c. golden raisins
15 dried apricots, finely cut up
8 tsp. butter
16 walnut halves
16 tsp. brown sugar

Cook and drain noodles. In mixer, combine butter, eggs, sugar, 3 tablespoons brown sugar, cinnamon, raisins and apricots. Mix with noodles in a large bowl. Grease muffin tins well and place ½ tsp. butter in the bottom of each cup. Place walnut half upside down on top of the butter and 1 tsp. of brown sugar on top of the walnut. Pat noodles firmly into each cup on top of the butter, nut and brown sugar. Bake at 350 degrees for 15-20 minutes. Watch carefully. Remove from oven and let stand 5 minutes. With a knife, loosen edges of noodle puddings. Invert and serve.

16 kugels

These freeze beautifully. To reheat, place thawed noodle puddings on cookie sheet and heat at 325 degrees for 10 minutes or until hot.

NOODLE KUGEL WITH LEMON SAUCE

Show ■
Go □

½ c. butter
8 oz. wide noodles,
   cooked and drained
8 oz. cream cheese,
   softened
¾ c. sugar
4 eggs
1 c. milk
dash of salt
1 tsp. vanilla
½ c. golden raisins
   (optional)

Topping:
1 c. crushed corn or bran
   flakes
¼ c. cinnamon-sugar

Lemon Sauce:
½-¾ c. lemon juice
1½ c. water
3 eggs, separated
1 c. sugar
2½ T. cornstarch
¼ c. cold water

Place butter on cooked noodles to melt. Whip cream cheese and sugar; add eggs (1 at a time), milk, salt and vanilla in blender or food processor. Add raisins if desired. Combine with noodles and spread in greased 9x13-inch pan. Top with crushed flakes and cinnamon-sugar. Bake at 350 degrees for 1 hour or until top is golden brown.

For lemon sauce, combine lemon juice, water, egg yolks, sugar and cornstarch that has been dissolved in cold water. Cook over low heat, stirring constantly until thick and smooth. Beat egg whites until stiff and fold by hand into completely cooled sauce. Refrigerate until needed.

12-14 servings

Even great without the lemon sauce.

a treasured recipe

CHEESE AND SPINACH PIE

Show ☐
Go ■

1 (10 oz.) pkg. frozen chopped spinach, cooked and drained
1 lb. Ricotta cheese
1 c. shredded Mozzarella, Feta or Cheddar cheese (or a combination)
3 eggs, slightly beaten
2 T. oil
½ tsp. onion salt
½ tsp. garlic salt
½ tsp. freshly ground pepper
10-inch frozen deep-dish pie crust
2 T. butter

Combine cooled spinach with cheeses, eggs, oil and seasonings. Pour into pie crust; dot with butter. Bake at 350 degrees for 40 minutes.

8 servings

May add sliced mushrooms, zucchini and green pepper if desired and bake in larger pie plate. Also may be made without crust.

MORE THAN A SPINACH RING

Show ■
Go ■

2 (10 oz.) pkgs. frozen chopped spinach, thawed and drained
1 lg. onion, chopped
¼ c. butter
½ lb. wide egg noodles
¼ lb. narrow egg noodles
16 oz. dairy sour cream
6 eggs, beaten
salt and pepper (needs a lot)

Press all water out of spinach. Sauté onion in butter until transparent. Cook noodles together in boiling water. Drain and let cool. Add to spinach and mix in sour cream, eggs, salt and pepper. Spoon into a greased 6½-cup ring mold; place in pan of hot water. Bake at 350 degrees for 1 hour.

6-8 servings

THE ORIGINAL CARROT RING

Show ■
Go ■

2¼ c. Spry
1½ c. brown sugar
3 eggs, separated
3 c. flour
3 tsp. baking powder
1½ tsp. baking soda
1½ tsp. salt
3 T. water
1 T. lemon juice
3 c. shredded carrots

Cream Spry and brown sugar together by hand. Add egg yolks and mix well. Mix flour, baking powder, soda and salt. Add to mixture alternately with water and lemon juice that has been mixed together. Add shredded carrots. Beat egg whites and fold into the mixture. Pour into 15-cup greased ring mold or springform pan. Bake at 350 degrees for 45-60 minutes.

12-14 servings

PUMPKIN MOLD

Show ■
Go ■

1½ c. flour
1⅓ c. sugar
¼ tsp. baking powder
1 tsp. baking soda
¾ tsp. salt
1 tsp. cinnamon
¼ tsp. nutmeg
⅓ c. shortening
⅓ c. chopped nuts
⅓ c. water
⅔ c. raisins
1 c. canned pumpkin
1 egg

Sift dry ingredients together into a large bowl. Add remaining ingredients and mix well. Pour into greased 6-cup ring mold. Bake at 350 degrees for 45 minutes. Let stand 15 minutes before unmolding.

6-8 servings

May double the recipe and bake in a bundt pan.

Break the common mold

Holiday Foods

THANKSGIVING BREAD STUFFING

Show ■
Go ☐

1 challah bread
1 lb. seasoned bread cubes
4 c. chopped celery
4 c. chopped onion
1 c. butter
¼ c. chicken fat
1 c. butter, melted
3 eggs, beaten
3 c. warm water
4 lg. potatoes, peeled and
   shredded
2 tsp. poultry seasoning
2 tsp. sage
1 tsp. each celery salt,
   thyme, salt and pepper

Dry challah by leaving it out uncovered overnight. Break it in small pieces and mix with bread cubes. Sauté celery and onion in 1 cup butter and add to bread mixture. Add remaining ingredients. Stuff the bird loosely with this moist mixture.

Place extra stuffing in a casserole and bake covered at 325 degrees for 2 hours.

Stuffing for 1 large turkey
plus extra casserole

CHOCOLATE CHIP MANDEL BROT

Show ■
Go ☐

½ c. butter or margarine
1 c. sugar
2 eggs
1 tsp. vanilla
1 tsp. almond extract
2 c. flour
1 tsp. baking powder
¼ tsp. cinnamon
½ c. chocolate chips
¼ c. sugar
½ tsp. cinnamon

Cream butter and sugar. Add eggs, vanilla and almond extract. Stir flour, baking powder and cinnamon into creamed mixture. Add chocolate chips and mix well. Using wet hands, divide dough into 3 parts. Make a loaf out of each and place on greased cookie sheet, leaving a few inches between each loaf. Bake at 350 degrees for 25-30 minutes. Remove from oven and slice each loaf in 6-8 pieces. Combine remaining sugar and cinnamon; sprinkle on slices. Return to oven and bake 5-10 minutes longer. Cool.

18-24 pieces

FROZEN PUMPKIN ICE CREAM PIE

Show ■
Go □

Crust:
¾ c. whole pitted dates
¼ c. water
¼ c. butter or margarine
1½ c. crushed corn flakes
1 T. sugar
⅓ c. chopped pecans

Filling:
1 pt. vanilla ice cream, softened
1 c. canned pumpkin
1¼ c. sugar
½ tsp. salt
¼ tsp. nutmeg
½ tsp. ginger
½ tsp. cinnamon
1 c. whipping cream

For crust, place dates and water in saucepan; cook over low heat, stirring frequently until paste is formed. Add butter, blend and cook until melted. Remove from heat; add corn flakes, sugar and nuts. Blend well. Press into bottom and side of 9-inch pie plate, using back of tablespoon.

For filling, line side of crust with ice cream. Blend together the pumpkin, sugar, salt, nutmeg, ginger and cinnamon. Whip and fold in cream and place mixture in crust and freeze at least 4 hours. Remove from freezer 15 minutes before serving. Garnish with additional whipped cream if desired.

8-10 servings

HOLIDAY HONEY CAKE

Show ■
Go □

3 eggs
1 c. sugar
2 tsp. baking soda
¾ c. cold coffee
1 c. honey
1 c. apricot preserves
¾ c. oil
1 tsp. cinnamon
1 tsp. allspice
½ tsp. salt
1 c. chopped nuts
juice and grated rind of 1 orange
1 apple, shredded with peel
3 c. flour

In large mixing bowl, cream eggs and sugar. Dissolve soda in coffee. Add honey, preserves, oil, spices, salt, nuts and coffee mixture to creamed mixture. Blend well. Add orange juice, rind and apple. Stir in flour and mix well. Line with waxed paper and grease a 15x4x4-inch or two 5x9-inch plus 1 mini size loaf pan and pour in mixture. Bake at 325 degrees for 40 minutes, then increase oven to 350 degrees and bake 20 minutes or until toothpick comes out clean. Let stand for a while before inverting pan. Remove waxed paper.

25 servings

CHAROSES FOR PASSOVER

Show ■
Go ■

¼ c. raisins
½ c. sherry
1 c. peeled, finely chopped
apple
1 lg. banana, cut in bite-
size pieces
¼ c. coarsely chopped
walnuts
¼ c. chopped dates
(optional)
1 tsp. honey
1 tsp. cinnamon
1-2 T. sweet red wine

Soak raisins in sherry overnight; refrigerate. When ready to use, drain and add remaining ingredients by hand.

2 cups

MOCK KISHKA FOR PASSOVER

Show ■
Go ■

1 (10 oz.) box egg matzo
crackers
2 lg. carrots
3 ribs celery
1 lg. onion
2 eggs
¾ c. butter or margarine,
melted
salt and pepper

Crush crackers in food processor. Empty bowl and finely chop all vegetables. Add butter and eggs; process until blended. Add crackers, salt and pepper and blend well. Form 2 rolls about 1½ inches in diameter and wrap tightly in foil. May be prepared in advance to this point and refrigerated or frozen until needed. (Thaw before baking.) Bake in foil on cookie sheet at 350 degrees for 45-50 minutes. Remove foil and slice in 2-inch slices.

16 slices

MATZO STUFFING

Show ■
Go ■

¾ c. minced onion
1½ c. coarsely chopped
   almonds
¼ lb. fresh mushrooms,
   sliced
¾ c. vegetable shortening
10 matzos, finely broken or
   7 c. matzo farfel
1 tsp. salt
¼ tsp. pepper
1 T. paprika
1 egg, beaten
2 c. clear chicken soup

Sauté onion, almonds and mushrooms in shortening until tender but not brown. Add matzos and cook 1 minute. Combine salt, pepper, paprika, egg and soup. Add to matzo mixture and mix well.

Stuffing for a 10-12 pound turkey

PASSOVER APPLE KUGEL

Show ■
Go ■

6 matzos
4 apples, peeled and cut
   into eighths
1½ c. raisins
½ tsp. cinnamon
rind of ½ lemon, grated
4-6 T. orange juice
1 c. sugar
¼ c. butter, melted
6 eggs, well beaten

Soak matzos in cold water until soft. Drain off water in colander. Combine matzos, apples, raisins, cinnamon, lemon rind, orange juice, sugar and butter. Add eggs; blend well. Pour into greased 9x13-inch pan. Bake at 350 degrees for 30-40 minutes.

16 servings

a rash of holiday ideas

PASSOVER ONION KUGEL

Show ■
Go ■

6 eggs, separated
2 c. finely chopped onions
⅓ c. peanut oil
⅓ c. matzo meal
1-1½ tsp. salt
¼ tsp. pepper

Grease a 2-quart casserole and place in 350 degree oven a few minutes to heat. Beat egg yolks until thick and creamy. Add onions, oil, matzo meal, salt and pepper; mix well. Beat egg whites until stiff. Fold into onion mixture, pour into casserole. Bake at 350 degrees for 30 minutes or until knife inserted in center comes out clean.

6 servings

SPINACH FRITTATA FOR PASSOVER

Show ■
Go ■

2 (10 oz.) pkgs. frozen
  chopped spinach,
  thawed and drained
6 eggs, beaten
1 c. grated Parmesan
  cheese
½ c. crumbled Feta cheese
  (or any mild cheese)
1 c. cottage cheese
¼ c. oil
⅓ c. matzo meal
¼ c. grated Parmesan
  cheese
yogurt or dairy sour cream

Place spinach in large mixing bowl. Add eggs and blend well. Add Parmesan, Feta and cottage cheese, oil and matzo meal, mixing thoroughly. Pour into greased 9x13-inch baking dish. Sprinkle with ¼ cup Parmesan cheese. Bake at 350 degrees for 1 hour. Cool slightly and cut into squares. Serve warm with yogurt or sour cream.

16 servings

May omit Feta cheese and just add ½ cup additional cottage cheese.

PASSOVER APPLE CARROT CASSEROLE

Show ■
Go ■

3 eggs, separated
½ c. butter or margarine, melted
¾ c. chopped almonds or pecans
1 lg. tart apple, shredded
1 c. shredded carrot
½ c. raisins
½ c. matzo meal
½ c. sugar
3 T. lemon juice
1 tsp. cinnamon

Beat egg whites until stiff. Set aside. Combine butter, nuts, yolks and remaining ingredients. Fold in egg whites. Pour into greased 2½-quart casserole. Bake at 375 degrees for 40 minutes.

5-6 servings

PASSOVER APPLE COFFEE CAKE

Show ■
Go □

¾ c. sugar
2 tsp. cinnamon
5 tart apples, peeled, cored and sliced
juice of 1 lemon
6 eggs
1¾ c. sugar
1 c. peanut oil
2 c. matzo cake meal
2 tsp. potato starch
dash salt
¼ c. sugar
2 tsp. cinnamon
¼ c. chopped walnuts

Combine ¾ cup sugar with 2 teaspoons cinnamon. Mix with sliced apples and lemon juice and set aside. Beat eggs with 1¾ cups sugar and add the oil. Sift together cake meal, potato starch and salt. Add to egg mixture, blending well. Pour half of batter into greased 9x13-inch cake pan. Spread apple mixture over batter. Top with rest of batter. Mix together remaining sugar and cinnamon with nuts and sprinkle over cake. Bake at 350 degrees for 1 hour and 15 minutes or until cake tests done.

24 squares

CHOCOLATE SOUFFLE FOR PASSOVER

Show ■
Go ☐

**7 (1 oz.) sq. semi-sweet
chocolate
¼ c. strong coffee
7 eggs, separated
¾ c. sugar**

**Chocolate Mocha Cream:
8 (1 oz.) sq. semi-sweet
chocolate
¼ c. strong coffee
1 c. plus 2 T. butter or
margarine, softened
1½ c. powdered sugar
4 eggs
2 T. cocoa**

**chocolate shavings
chopped nuts**

Celebrate!

Melt 7 ounces chocolate and ¼ cup coffee. Cool slightly. Beat egg yolks with ½ cup sugar until fluffy and lemon colored. Add chocolate and coffee mixture. In separate bowl, beat egg whites until soft peaks form. Add ¼ cup sugar, gradually beating until stiff peaks form. Gently fold egg whites into chocolate. Spread batter into greased 10½x15½-inch jelly roll pan that has been lined with greased waxed paper. Bake at 350 degrees for 15-20 minutes or until firm. Remove and cool for 5 minutes. Place a damp cloth over roll and set in a cool place.

For chocolate mocha cream, melt chocolate in coffee, stirring constantly; let cool. Cream butter and sugar and add to chocolate mixture, blending well. Add eggs, one at a time, and beat until smooth. Remove roll from pan onto fresh piece of waxed paper. When ready to use, remove towel and sprinkle roll with cocoa. Spread half of the mocha filling over top and roll up starting at long end. Frost with remaining filling. Decorate top with shavings and nuts. Slice and serve. Refrigerate any leftover roll.

12 servings

If roll is too long, cut to fit size of serving plate.

PASSOVER CHOCOLATE CHIFFON CAKE

Show ■
Go ■

⅔ c. cold water
¼ c. cocoa
8 lg. eggs, separated
1½ c. sugar
½ c. oil
½ c. matzo cake meal
½ c. potato starch

Boil water and cocoa together until slightly thickened. Let cool. Beat egg whites, add ¼ cup sugar and beat until stiff. Set aside. Beat yolks and remaining 1¼ cup sugar together. Add chocolate mixture, oil, cake meal and starch. Mix well. Fold in whites. Pour into ungreased 10-inch angel food pan. Bake at 325 degrees for 10 minutes. Increase heat to 350 degrees and bake for 50 minutes. Invert to cool. Before removing from pan, run knife around cake to loosen the sides.

10-12 servings

PASSOVER CHOCOLATE CAKE

Show ■
Go ■

6 oz. semi-sweet chocolate
10 eggs, separated
¾ c. plus 2 T. sugar
2 c. finely chopped walnuts

Melt chocolate; cool. Beat egg yolks and sugar until thick and lemon colored. Stir in chocolate and fold in chopped nuts. Beat egg whites until stiff, but not dry; fold into chocolate mixture. Pour batter into a greased 10-inch springform pan. Bake at 350 degrees for 1 hour or until center springs back when lightly touched. Cool completely; remove side of pan. Serve plain or with Fudge Sauce (see index) and whipped cream.

10-12 servings

Don't pass over this one!

PASSOVER ANGEL FOOD CAKE

Show ■
Go ■

10 lg. egg whites
¼ tsp. salt
1 T. lemon juice
2 T. orange juice
¾ c. sugar
¾ c. potato starch
¼ c. cake meal
¾ c. sugar

Beat egg whites until foamy. Add salt and juices. Beat until very thick. Gradually add ¾ cup sugar and beat until mixture forms peaks. Sift together potato starch, cake meal and ¾ cup sugar; fold into egg white mixture. Pour into 10-inch angel food pan. Bake at 350 degrees for 45-50 minutes. Invert to cool. Before removing from pan, run knife around cake to loosen the sides.

10-12 servings

PASSOVER BROWNIES

Show ■
Go ■

1 c. sugar
½ c. butter, melted
¼ c. cocoa
2 eggs, separated and
    beaten
¼ c. milk
¼ tsp. salt
½ c. matzo cake meal
powdered sugar

Combine sugar, butter and cocoa together. Add beaten egg yolks, milk, salt and cake meal. Fold in beaten egg whites. Pour into greased 8x8-inch pan. Bake at 350 degrees for 30 minutes. Dust with powdered sugar.

1-1½ dozen bars

Good enough to make all year long.

MATZO BALLS FOR PASSOVER

Show ■
Go ■

3 eggs, separated
½ tsp. salt
¾ c. matzo meal

Beat egg whites until stiff. In separate bowl beat egg yolks. Fold yolks into whites. Add salt to matzo meal and add to egg mixture. Refrigerate for 15 minutes. Wet hands and shape loosely into small balls. Drop into a very large pot of rapidly boiling salted water and cook for 45 minutes. Keep covered the entire time. Remove and add to hot soup.

14 matzo balls

PESACH PUDDING

Show ■
Go ■

¾ c. seedless raisins
1 lemon
4 cooking apples
4 eggs, separated
¼ tsp. salt
1 c. sugar
½ c. matzo meal
½ tsp. cinnamon

Rinse and drain raisins. Grate rind from lemon and squeeze juice. Peel and chop apples into small chunks. Add lemon rind and juice to apples. Beat egg whites with salt until stiff. Gradually beat in sugar. Beat yolks well and fold into egg whites. Fold in matzo meal, raisins, cinnamon and apples. Pour into greased 9x13-inch baking dish. Bake at 350 degrees for 30 minutes. Serve warm or cold.

12 servings

MOM'S HAMANTASHEN

Show ■
Go □

Dough:
1 c. sugar
1 c. butter or margarine,
   softened
3 eggs
½ tsp. salt
rind of 1 orange
¼ c. orange juice
1 tsp. vanilla
4 c. flour
3 tsp. baking powder

Filling:
8 oz. pitted prunes
8 oz. dried apricots
¼ c. raisins
¼ c. nuts (optional)
⅛ c. lemon juice
¼ tsp. cinnamon
1 (6 oz.) jar strawberry jam

For dough, using a mixer, cream together sugar and butter. Add eggs and mix well. Add remaining ingredients in order listed. Cover with waxed paper and refrigerate for several hours.

For filling, grind together prunes, apricots, raisins and nuts. Add lemon juice, cinnamon and jam. Mix thoroughly.

To assemble, roll out ½ of dough on floured board. Cut into 1½-inch rounds with cookie cutter. Put a small amount of filling in center of each circle. Fold over and pinch together in triangular form. Place on greased cookie sheet. Sprinkle with sugar. Bake at 350 degrees for 20-30 minutes or until browned.

4 dozen

WHOLE WHEAT HAMANTASHEN

Show ■
Go □

Dough:
½ c. butter or margarine
½ c. sugar
¼ c. honey
1 tsp. vanilla
1 tsp. vinegar
2 eggs
1½ c. whole wheat flour
1½ c. all-purpose flour
2 tsp. baking powder
1 tsp. cinnamon
½ tsp. baking soda

Raisin Poppy Seed Filling:
5 T. poppy seeds
¾ c. raisins
1½ T. honey
2 T. butter, melted
2 tsp. grated lemon rind

Apricot Filling:
½ c. finely chopped dried
　apricots
½ c. finely chopped
　almonds or walnuts
1½ T. honey
2 T. melted butter
¼ tsp. cinnamon or ginger

For dough, in large bowl, beat together butter, sugar, honey, vanilla, vinegar and eggs until well mixed. In small bowl, mix flours, baking powder, cinnamon and soda. Add to sugar mixture and blend well. Chill at least 3 hours or overnight.

Choose one filling; mix all ingredients together in small bowl. On a well floured board, roll dough to ⅛-inch thickness and cut into 3-inch circles. Set circles slightly apart on lightly greased baking sheets. Drop a generous teaspoon of one of the fillings onto center of each circle. Bring edges up to form a triangle and pinch seams together to seal. Re-roll scraps and repeat process until dough and filling are used. Bake at 350 degrees for about 15 minutes or until edges are brown. Cool on wire rack. Store in airtight container. These freeze well.

2 dozen

Healthy days are here again!

Sweet Stuff

SPICY RAISIN BARS

Show ■
Go ■

1 c. raisins
1 c. water
½ c. oil
1 c. sugar
1 egg, slightly beaten
1¾ c. flour
¼ tsp. salt
1 tsp. baking soda
1 tsp. cinnamon
1 tsp. nutmeg
½ tsp. cloves
½ c. chopped nuts

Frosting:
2 c. powdered sugar
¼ c. butter, melted
lemon juice

Combine raisins, water and oil and bring to a boil. Cool to lukewarm. Stir in sugar and egg. Sift dry ingredients together and add to raisin mixture. Fold in nuts. Pour into greased 9x13-inch pan. Bake at 350 degrees for 25 minutes or until bars spring back when lightly touched. Cool. For frosting, in a small bowl, mix powdered sugar and butter. Add enough lemon juice to make smooth spreading consistency and frost bars.

32 bars

a real raisin for living

OATMEAL CARAMEL SQUARES

Show ■
Go ■

3 c. flour
3 c. quick oatmeal
2¼ c. brown sugar
1½ tsp. baking soda
¾ tsp. salt
2 c. butter, melted
3 c. chocolate chips
1½ c. chopped pecans
2 (12 oz.) jars caramel ice cream topping
6 T. flour

Mix 3 cups flour, oatmeal, brown sugar, soda and salt with butter. Press half the mixture into a greased 11½x16-inch jelly roll pan. Bake at 350 degrees for 10 minutes. Sprinkle with chocolate chips and pecans. Mix caramel topping with 6 tablespoons flour and drizzle over chips. Sprinkle remaining batter on top and pat down. Put pan on a large cookie sheet. Bake at 350 degrees for 20 minutes. Cool and cut into 1-inch squares.

80 squares

GRAHAM CRACKER GOODY BARS

Show ■
Go ■

2¼ c. graham cracker
   crumbs
1 (6 oz.) pkg. chocolate
   chips
1 (14 oz.) can sweetened
   condensed milk
1 tsp. vanilla
powdered sugar

Mix graham cracker crumbs, chocolate chips, milk and vanilla together by hand. Spread in a greased 8x8-inch pan. Bake at 350 degrees for 20 minutes. Let stand until partially cooled. Cut into squares and roll in powdered sugar. Bars must be slightly warm or sugar will not stick. For a double recipe use a 9x13-inch pan.

16 bars

MIXED NUT BARS

Show ■
Go ■

1½ c. flour
½ c. butter, softened
¾ c. sugar
½ tsp. salt
1 (6 oz.) pkg. butterscotch
   chips
½ c. light corn syrup
2 T. butter
1 T. water
1 (12½ oz.) can mixed nuts

Mix flour, butter, sugar and salt together and press into an ungreased 9x13-inch pan. Bake at 350 degrees for 10 minutes. In a saucepan, combine chips, syrup, butter and water. Heat until chips are melted. Pour over baked crust. Sprinkle mixed nuts over the top and bake another 10 minutes. Cut while warm.

24 bars

goody goody for everyone!

HERSHEY BAR BARS

Show ■
Go ■

1 c. unsalted butter
¾ c. sugar
1 egg
2 tsp. vanilla
½ tsp. salt
2½ c. flour
3 (8 oz.) Hershey chocolate
    bars
powdered sugar

With hand mixer or food processor, cream butter and sugar. Add egg, vanilla, salt and flour; blend. Press half of dough into a greased 9x13-inch pan. Place chocolate bars on top. Pat remaining dough over bars and make ridges with a fork. Bake at 350 degrees for 25-35 minutes or until edges are brown and top remains light. Cut while warm. Remove from pan and sprinkle with powdered sugar.

24 bars

LEMON SOUR WALNUT BARS

Show ■
Go ■

Crust:
¾ c. flour
⅓ c. butter, softened

Filling:
1 c. brown sugar
½ tsp. vanilla
2 eggs
¾ c. flaked coconut,
    packed
⅛ tsp. baking powder
½ c. chopped walnuts

Glaze:
⅔ c. powdered sugar
1 T. grated lemon rind
2 T. lemon juice

For crust, blend flour and butter. Press into an ungreased 8x8-inch pan. Bake at 350 degrees for 12 minutes. Combine all filling ingredients and pour into crust. Continue to bake for 25 minutes. Cool. For glaze, mix powdered sugar and lemon rind. Slowly stir in lemon juice to glaze consistency and pour over bars.

16 bars

DATE SQUARES

Show ■
Go ■

1½ c. flour
1½ c. quick oatmeal
½ c. butter or Crisco
1 tsp. baking soda
¾ c. brown sugar
¼ tsp. salt
1 (8 oz.) pkg. chopped
   dates
¾ c. sugar
¾ c. water
½ tsp. vanilla

Combine flour, oatmeal, butter, soda, brown sugar and salt with a fork. In a greased 8x8-inch pan, pat down half of the mixture. In medium saucepan, boil dates, sugar and water for a few minutes until dates are soft; add vanilla. Pour date mixture over dough. Sprinkle remaining dough on top and pat down. Bake at 350 degrees for 20 minutes. Cool and cut into squares.

16 squares

CARROT BARS

Show ■
Go ■

4 eggs
2 c. sugar
1½ c. oil
2 c. flour
2 tsp. baking soda
1 tsp. salt
1 T. cinnamon
3 (4½ oz.) jars strained
   carrot baby food

Frosting:
¼ c. butter, melted
1 (8 oz.) pkg. cream
   cheese, softened
½ tsp. vanilla
3½-4 c. powdered sugar

In mixer bowl, beat eggs until thick. Gradually add sugar, oil, flour, soda, salt and cinnamon; mix well. Add carrots. Pour into greased 10½x15½-inch jelly roll pan. Bake at 350 degrees for 30-40 minutes. Cool. Do not overbake.

For frosting, mix together butter, cream cheese and vanilla. Slowly beat in powdered sugar until spreading consistency. Spread on cooled bars.

75 bars

a taste for sore eyes!

EDINER SUPER BROWNIES

Show ■
Go ■

1 c. flour
1 tsp. baking powder
1 tsp. salt
⅔ c. butter
5 (1 oz.) sq. unsweetened
  chocolate
2 c. sugar
4 eggs, slightly beaten
2 tsp. vanilla
1½ c. chopped nuts

Frosting:
2 (1 oz.) sq. unsweetened
  chocolate
⅓ c. butter
1½ c. powdered sugar
¼ c. hot coffee

In a bowl, mix together flour, baking powder and salt. Set aside. In a large saucepan over low heat, melt butter and chocolate. Blend in sugar, eggs, vanilla and flour mixture until well combined. Stir in nuts. Pour into greased 9x13-inch pan. Bake at 350 degrees for 20-25 minutes, until center has just set. Cool completely before frosting.

For frosting, melt chocolate and butter over low heat. Stir in sugar and coffee. Beat until smooth. Let cool before spreading on brownies.

24 bars

NEW YORK, NEW YORK BROWNIES

Show ■
Go ■

2 (1 oz.) sq. unsweetened
  chocolate
1 c. butter
2 eggs
1 c. sugar
½ c. flour
½ tsp. vanilla
½ c. chopped pecans

Melt chocolate and butter together; cool. Mix eggs and sugar. Add melted chocolate mixture. Mix in flour, vanilla and pecans; pour into greased 8x8-inch pan. Bake at 350 degrees for 25-30 minutes. Cut while warm.

16 bars

Enjoy... Enjoy... ENJOY!

FILTHY RICH BROWNIES

Show ■
Go ■

2 eggs
1 c. sugar
1 tsp. vanilla
½ c. butter
2 (1 oz.) sq. unsweetened
  chocolate
½ c. chocolate chips
½ c. flour

Frosting:
¼ c. butter, softened
2 c. powdered sugar
¼ c. milk
⅓ c. cocoa
1 tsp. vanilla

Beat eggs until thick and lemon colored. Gradually add sugar and continue to beat. Add vanilla. In double boiler or microwave melt butter and chocolates. Let cool a few minutes. Combine chocolate and egg mixtures. Fold in flour. Pour into greased 9x9-inch pan. Bake at 350 degrees for 20 minutes. Cool.

For frosting, place frosting ingredients in mixer and blend until smooth. Spread on brownies. If food processor is used, make frosting with cold butter.

16-18 bars

FUDGIE BROWNIES

Show ■
Go ■

1 c. Crisco
4 (1 oz.) sq. unsweetened
  chocolate
2 c. sugar
4 eggs
1 c. flour
1 tsp. salt
1 T. vanilla
1 c. miniature
  marshmallows
1 c. walnuts, in large pieces
1 c. chocolate chips
  (optional)
powdered sugar

Melt Crisco and chocolate together. Mix in sugar and let cool. With wooden spoon, stir in eggs, flour, salt and vanilla. Fold in marshmallows and nuts; add chocolate chips if desired. Place in greased 9x13-inch pan and bake at 350 degrees for 20-25 minutes. Do not overbake. Sprinkle with powdered sugar.

36 bars

DOUBLE FEATURE BROWNIES

Show ■
Go □

1 (4 oz.) pkg. German's
   sweet chocolate
3 T. butter
1 (3 oz.) pkg. cream
   cheese, softened
2 T. butter, softened
1 c. sugar
3 eggs
1 T. flour
1½ tsp. vanilla
½ tsp. baking powder
¼ tsp. salt
½ c. flour
¼ tsp. almond extract
¼ tsp. butter extract
½ c. nuts

Frosting:
½ c. chocolate chips
2 T. butter
¼ tsp. almond extract
3 T. milk
1 c. powdered sugar, sifted

chocolate shot (optional)

Melt chocolate and 3 tablespoons butter over low heat. Let cool. Mix cream cheese with 2 tablespoons butter. Slowly add ¼ cup sugar and blend thoroughly. Add 1 egg, 1 tablespoon flour and ¼ teaspoon vanilla. Set aside. In bowl, beat remaining eggs and slowly add remaining sugar. Mix well. Add baking powder, salt and ½ cup flour. Add the chocolate mixture, remaining vanilla, almond and butter extracts. Stir in nuts.

Grease and flour an 8x8-inch pan and pour in ½ of mixture. Cover with cream cheese batter and spoon on remaining chocolate mixture. Marble with knife. Bake at 350 degrees for 35-40 minutes.

For frosting, in saucepan over low heat, combine chocolate chips, butter, almond extract and milk. Stir until chocolate is melted. Remove from heat. Stir in powdered sugar and beat until glossy and easy to spread. Frost brownies and sprinkle with chocolate shot. Recipe may be doubled and baked in 9x13-inch pan.

16 bars

Be careful, it's easy to O.D. on these!

YUM YUM COOKIES

Show ■
Go ■

1 c. butter, softened
1 c. brown sugar
1 c. sugar
2 eggs
2 tsp. vanilla
½ c. raisins or chopped
   dates
½ c. chopped walnuts
½ c. flaked coconut
2 c. quick oatmeal
2 c. flour
1 tsp. salt
1 tsp. baking soda

Cream butter and sugars. Add eggs, vanilla, dates, walnuts and coconut. Stir in remaining ingredients. Drop by teaspoonfuls onto greased cookie sheet. Flatten with glass dipped in sugar. Bake at 350 degrees for 10 minutes.

8 dozen

CHOCOLATE DIPPED TREATS

Show ■
Go □

1 c. butter, softened
¾ c. powdered sugar
1 tsp. vanilla
2 c. flour

Frosting:
2 (1 oz.) sq. unsweetened
   chocolate
2 c. powdered sugar
drops of milk

Cream butter, sugar and vanilla. Add flour and blend well. Shape dough into crescent shapes or round balls. Bake on ungreased cookie sheet at 350 degrees for 15 minutes. Cool on rack.

For frosting, melt chocolate in double boiler. Mix in powdered sugar. Add a few drops of milk until frosting is desired consistency for dipping. Dip end or top of each cookie into chocolate and let stand on rack to cool.

To vary, sprinkle chopped nuts, chocolate or colored sprinkles on freshly dipped cookies.

4-5 dozen

OATMEAL CHOCOLATE CHIP COOKIES

Show ☐
Go ■

½ c. vegetable shortening
½ c. butter or margarine, softened
¾ c. brown sugar
¾ c. sugar
2 eggs, slightly beaten
1½ tsp. vanilla
1 T. hot water
2 c. flour
1½ tsp. baking soda
½ tsp. salt
1 c. chocolate chips
1½ c. quick oatmeal
1 c. chopped walnuts

Cream shortening, butter and sugars. Add eggs. Stir in vanilla and water. Sift together flour, baking soda and salt and add to creamed mixture. Stir in chocolate chips, oatmeal and nuts. Drop by teaspoonfuls onto ungreased cookie sheets. Bake at 350 degrees for 8-10 minutes or until light brown.

4-5 dozen

OATMEAL CRISPS

Show ■
Go ■

3 c. packed brown sugar
6 c. quick oatmeal
3 c. butter, softened
1 T. baking soda
3 c. flour

Place all ingredients in a large bowl. Knead by hand into a well packed firm dough. Refrigerate for 30 minutes. Shape into small balls. Place on ungreased cookie sheet. Flatten with glass dipped in sugar. Bake at 350 degrees for 10-12 minutes.

13 dozen

May be half-dipped in melted chocolate for fancy occasion.

So nice to come home to!

MY MOM'S CINNAMON COOKIES

Show ■
Go ■

3 eggs
¾ c. brown sugar
1 c. oil
1 tsp. baking powder
¼ tsp. baking soda
2½ c. flour
¼ tsp. salt
1 tsp. vanilla
½ c. sugar
1 tsp. cinnamon

Beat eggs. Add sugar and oil; continue beating. Mix in baking powder, soda, flour, salt and vanilla. Dough will be stiff. Oil hands and shape dough into small balls. Roll in mixture of sugar and cinnamon. Place on greased cookie sheet. Bake at 350 degrees for 10 minutes. These freeze well.

5 dozen

COOKIE BRITTLE

Show ■
Go ■

1 c. butter or margarine
1½ tsp. vanilla
1 tsp. salt
1 c. sugar
2 c. flour
1 (6 oz.) pkg. chocolate
   chips
½ c. finely chopped nuts
powdered sugar

In mixer or food processor, cream butter, vanilla, salt and sugar. Add flour. Mix in chocolate chips by hand. Pat into ungreased 10½x15½-inch jelly roll pan. Sprinkle nuts on top. Bake at 375 degrees for 20-25 minutes or until lightly browned. Cool. Break into irregular pieces and drain on absorbent paper. Dust with powdered sugar.

20-30 pieces

SESAME CRESCENTS

Show ■
Go □

6 T. sugar
6 T. oil
2 eggs, beaten
6 T. flour
2½ c. sesame seeds

Mix together all ingredients and refrigerate for 3 hours. Divide dough in half and place on waxed paper. Using wet hands, roll dough into strips ½ inch in diameter. Cut strips into 1½-inch pieces. Shape into crescents and place on foil-lined cookie sheets. Bake at 350 degrees for 15-20 minutes or until brown.

5-6 dozen

POPPY SEED COOKIES

Show ☐
Go ■

½ c. butter, softened
½ c. sugar
¼ tsp. vanilla
1 egg
2 c. flour
½ tsp. baking powder
¼ c. poppy seeds

Cream butter, sugar and vanilla. Add egg, flour, baking powder and poppy seeds. Blend well. Divide dough into 2 equal parts and roll into logs 1½ inches in diameter. Wrap each log in waxed paper and place in freezer. When firm, slice thinly and place on greased or teflon cookie sheets. Bake at 375 degrees for 10-15 minutes. Watch carefully.

5½ dozen

APPLE STRUDEL

Show ■
Go ☐

5-6 firm apples, peeled and
  thinly sliced
2 tsp. cinnamon
¼ c. sugar
1 c. brown sugar
½ c. golden raisins
4 oz. chopped pecans
1 pkg. fillo strudel leaves
1 c. butter, melted
graham cracker crumbs, for
  sprinkling
1 (16 oz.) jar cherry
  preserves

Place apples in large bowl. Add cinnamon, sugars, raisins and nuts. Mix well. For 1 strudel roll, unfold fillo leaves and place 1 leaf on a towel. Cover remaining leaves with moist towel. Brush leaf with butter and sprinkle with cracker crumbs. Place a second leaf on top and repeat butter and crumbs process until there are 6 fillo sheets.

With slotted spoon, take ⅓ of apple mixture and place on long end of leaf. Put ⅓ of cherry preserves along top of apple mixture. Roll up like jelly roll; brush with butter and place on buttered jelly roll pan. Repeat for two more rolls. Make slits 2 inches apart on top. Bake at 375 degrees for 35 minutes. Slice and serve warm with ice cream.

Freezes well in foil. To serve, thaw in refrigerator overnight. Place on jelly roll pan and open foil. Heat at 325 degrees about 20 minutes.

3 rolls, 6-8 servings per roll

SPONGE CAKE WITH LEMON FILLING

Show ■
Go □

6 eggs, separated
1 c. sugar
¼ c. cold water
1 tsp. lemon extract
1 tsp. grated lemon rind
1 c. sifted cake flour
½ tsp. cream of tartar
½ tsp. salt

Filling and Frosting:
1 c. sugar
3 T. cornstarch
½ tsp. salt
1 c. water
2 T. grated lemon rind
½ c. lemon juice
2 T. butter
4 egg yolks
coconut

Beat 6 egg yolks until thick, at least 5 minutes. Gradually beat in sugar. Combine water, lemon extract and rind; beat alternately with flour into yolks. In large bowl, beat 6 egg whites, cream of tartar and salt until stiff. Gently fold yolk mixture into whites and pour into ungreased 10-inch tube pan. Bake at 325 degrees for 60-65 minutes. When cake springs back when touched lightly on top, invert until completely cool.

For filling, mix sugar, cornstarch, salt, water, lemon rind, juice and butter in saucepan. Bring to rolling boil and boil 1 minute, stirring constantly. Remove from heat and beat in egg yolks. Return to heat and cook 1 minute more, stirring constantly. Chill. Cut cake into 2 layers and spread with filling. Frost sides and top. Sprinkle with coconut.

10-12 servings

GATEAU CHOCOLAT

Show ■
Go □

15 oz. Tobler bittersweet
chocolate bars
14 T. butter
10 eggs, separated
1½ c. sugar
2 T. Grand Marnier liqueur
2 tsp. vanilla
powdered sugar
whipped cream

Melt chocolate and butter together. Add egg yolks, sugar, liqueur and vanilla. Beat egg whites until stiff and gently fold into mixture. Pour into a well greased 10-inch springform pan. Bake at 275 degrees for 2¼ hours. Cake will rise and fall during baking and crumble when crust is cut. Sprinkle with powdered sugar and serve warm with dab of whipped cream.

16 servings

FRANGELICO RUM CAKE

Show ■
Go □

1 c. chopped nuts
2 T. sugar
1 (3¾ oz.) pkg. instant
  vanilla pudding
4 eggs
½ c. water
½ c. oil
¼ c. rum
¼ c. Frangelico or
  Amaretto liqueur
1 (18 oz.) pkg. yellow cake
  mix

Syrup:
½ c. butter
¼ c. water
1 c. sugar
¼ c. rum
¼ c. Frangelico or
  Amaretto liqueur

Mix nuts and 2 tablespoons sugar. Sprinkle in bottom of well greased and floured bundt pan. Blend in mixer for 5 minutes or food processor for 1 minute, the pudding, eggs, water, oil, rum and liqueur. Add cake mix and blend well in mixer or until it is completely blended in processor. Pour into bundt pan. Bake at 325 degrees for 1 hour. Leave in pan. While warm, poke lots of holes with a fork in cake.

For syrup, combine butter, water and sugar in medium saucepan. Boil 5 minutes, stirring constantly. Add rum and Frangelico. Pour hot syrup over cake. Cool cake completely in pan before removing.

10-12 servings

RHUBARB CAKE

Show ■
Go ■

1½ c. brown sugar
½ c. butter or margarine,
  softened
1 egg
2 c. flour
½ tsp. salt
1 tsp. baking soda
1 c. buttermilk
3 c. diced rhubarb
1 c. chopped nuts
½ c. sugar
2 tsp. cinnamon

In mixing bowl, cream sugar and butter. Add egg. Combine flour, salt and soda; add alternately with buttermilk to creamed mixture. Stir in rhubarb and nuts. Pour into 9x13-inch pan. Combine sugar and cinnamon and sprinkle on top. Bake at 350 degrees for 40 minutes. May be served warm or cold. Freezes well.

24 servings

CHOCOLATE TOFFEE CAKE

Show ■
Go ■

1 (10-inch) angel food cake

Toffee:
1 c. butter
1 c. sugar
**1 c. whole blanched
    almonds**

Frosting:
½ c. butter
2 c. powdered sugar
4 eggs
1 tsp. vanilla
**8 oz. bittersweet
    chocolate, melted**

Cut cake into 3 layers. For toffee, slowly melt 1 cup butter and 1 cup sugar in saucepan. Increase heat; add almonds and stir until mixed. Continue to cook and stir about 10 minutes or until coffee colored. Watch carefully. Pour into ungreased 8x10-inch pan; cool. Chop into bite-size pieces when hard.

For frosting, cream butter and powdered sugar; mix in eggs one at a time. Stir in vanilla and melted chocolate; beat until mixed. Add more powdered sugar if frosting is too thin.

Spread frosting on bottom layer of cake and sprinkle generously with toffee pieces. Place second cake layer on top and repeat process. Add third layer and frost entire cake top and sides. Sprinkle remaining toffee over cake.

12-14 servings

May substitute crushed Heath or Almond Roca bars for toffee as a time saver.

TEXAS CHOCOLATE SHEET CAKE

Show ■
Go ■

2 c. sugar
2 c. flour
½ tsp. salt
1 c. butter
1 c. water
3 T. cocoa
½ c. dairy sour cream
2 eggs
1 tsp. baking soda
dash of cinnamon

Frosting:
¼ c. butter or shortening
⅓ c. cocoa
2 c. powdered sugar
¼ c. milk
1 tsp. vanilla

In a large bowl, combine sugar, flour and salt; set aside. In a small saucepan, bring butter, water and cocoa to a boil. Remove from heat. Add to dry ingredients and mix well. Add sour cream, eggs, soda and cinnamon and blend well. Pour into greased and lightly floured 10½x15½-inch jelly roll pan. Bake at 375 degrees for 20-25 minutes. Do not overbake. For frosting, melt butter and cocoa together. Add remaining ingredients and blend until smooth. Spread on cake.

40 pieces

Looks like a brownie, tastes like a cake

CHEESECAKE SUPREME

Show ■
Go ■

Crust:
3 c. graham cracker crumbs
½ c. sugar
½ c. butter, melted

Filling:
5 (8 oz.) pkg. cream cheese
1 (3 oz.) pkg. cream cheese
1½ c. sugar
5 eggs
2 c. sour cream
1½ tsp. vanilla
juice of one lemon

For crust, mix together graham cracker crumbs, ½ cup sugar and butter. Press into bottom of 10½-inch springform pan. For filling, in a large bowl at medium speed, beat together cream cheese, 1½ cup sugar and eggs for 15 minutes. Add sour cream, vanilla and lemon juice. Beat an additional 15 minutes. Pour into prepared pan. Bake at 350 degrees for 55 minutes. Turn off oven and let cheesecake remain in oven for 2 hours. Remove and cool. Refrigerate.

12 Servings

CHOCOLATE SWIRL CHEESECAKE

Show ■
Go ■

Crust:
4½ oz. chocolate cookie wafers
2 T. sugar
1 tsp. cinnamon
¼ c. unsalted butter, melted

Filling:
1 (6 oz.) pkg. chocolate chips
3 (8 oz.) pkgs. cream cheese, softened
4 lg. eggs
1 c. sugar
1 tsp. vanilla

In food processor or blender, crumble the wafers. Add sugar, cinnamon and butter; mix well. Press mixture into a greased 8-inch springform pan and set aside.

For filling, melt chocolate. In large mixing bowl or food processor, cream the cheese. Add eggs and blend. Slowly add sugar, then vanilla and blend thoroughly. Pour all but 3 tablespoons batter into crust. Mix melted chocolate with remaining batter to form a stiff paste. Drop dollops of chocolate mixture on top of cheesecake batter. Swirl by running a knife through and around in zigzag motion.

With aluminum foil, make a collar about 3 inches high. Fit around edge of pan, pinching to attach to edge and bend collar in a little to protect cheesecake. Bake at 375 degrees for 1¼-1½ hours. Cheesecake is done when it has risen, is firm in center and has cracked around edge. Remove from oven, let cool and refrigerate overnight in springform pan. Before serving, remove springform and drizzle top with melted chocolate, if desired.

10-12 servings

oohs and ahs!

PRALINE CHEESECAKE

Show ■
Go ■

Crust:
1 c. graham cracker crumbs
3 T. sugar
3 T. butter, melted

Filling:
**3 (8 oz.) pkgs. cream
cheese, softened**
1½ c. dark brown sugar
2 T. flour
3 eggs
1½ tsp. vanilla
½ c. finely chopped pecans

maple syrup
pecans, coarsely broken

Mix cracker crumbs with sugar and butter. Blend well and press into 9-inch springform pan. Bake at 350 degrees for 10 minutes. For filling, combine cream cheese, sugar and flour until well blended. Beat in eggs, one at a time. Add vanilla and nuts. Pour over crust and bake at 350 degrees for 50-55 minutes. Cake will pull away from sides and top will crack. May be frozen at this point. Brush top with lots of syrup, letting it fill cracks. Cover with broken pecans.

12-14 servings

CHOCOLATE CHEESECAKE

Show ■
Go □

Crust:
**1 (9 oz.) pkg. chocolate
cookie wafers, crushed**
¼ c. butter, melted

Filling:
**4 (8 oz.) pkgs. cream
cheese, softened**
1 c. sugar
4 eggs
**2 (1 oz.) sq. semi-sweet
chocolate**
1 T. butter

½ pt. whipping cream
2 T. powdered sugar
½ tsp. vanilla
chocolate curls

For crust, combine wafers and melted butter and press onto side and bottom of a greased 10-inch springform pan. Chill while preparing filling.

For filling, blend 8 ounces cream cheese with ¼ cup sugar and 1 egg in food processor or mixer. Repeat this process three times, beating well after each addition. Melt chocolate and butter and add to creamed mixture; pour over cooled crust. Bake at 350 degrees for 25-30 minutes. Turn off heat, leave oven door half open for 30 minutes. Remove cheesecake from oven and cool. Whip cream with powdered sugar and vanilla. Spread over cream cheese layer and garnish with chocolate curls.

16 servings

COCONUT CUSTARD PIE

Show ■
Go ■

1 c. freshly grated coconut or 1 (3½ oz.) can flaked coconut
3 eggs
¼ c. butter, softened
½ c. flour
½ tsp. baking powder
1 c. sugar
¼ tsp. salt
1 tsp. vanilla
1 tsp. grated lime rind
2 c. milk
3 T. coconut rum (or 1 T. cream of coconut with 2 T. white rum)

Place all ingredients in blender and process until combined. Pour mixture into a 10-inch greased pie plate and bake at 350 degrees for 1 hour. Sprinkle coconut and chocolate shavings on top if desired. Chill and serve.

12 servings

CHOCOLATE CHIP PECAN PIE

Show ■
Go ■

1 c. sugar
4 eggs
1 c. light corn syrup
1 tsp. vanilla
½ c. butter
1 c. chopped pecans
1 (6 oz.) pkg. chocolate chips
1 unbaked 10-inch pie shell, regular or graham cracker

Combine sugar, eggs, syrup, vanilla and mix well. Melt butter, cool and add to mixture. Fold in pecans and chocolate chips, stirring until well mixed. Pour into pie shell. Bake at 350 degrees for 50-60 minutes or until set.

6-8 servings

BUSTER BAR DESSERT

Show ■
Go ■

1 lb. Oreo cookies
½ c. butter or margarine, melted
½ gal. vanilla ice cream, softened
1½ c. Spanish peanuts
2 c. powdered sugar
⅔ c. chocolate chips
1½ c. evaporated milk
½ c. butter
1 tsp. vanilla

Crush cookies in food processor or with rolling pin. Mix cookies with ½ cup butter and pat in 9x13-inch pan. Spread ice cream over cookies. Top with peanuts. Freeze. Combine powdered sugar, chocolate chips, milk and ½ cup butter in a saucepan. Slowly bring to boil and simmer 8 minutes, stirring constantly. Remove from heat and add vanilla. Cool and spread over ice cream and nuts. Freeze until ready to serve.

12 servings

Rx for a rainy day

COOKIE SUNDAE PIE

Show ■
Go ☐

Shell:
3 egg whites
pinch of salt
¾ c. sugar
12 Oreo cookies, crushed
½ c. chopped pecans
¼ tsp. vanilla
pinch of cream of tartar

Filling:
½ gal. ice cream, favorite flavor
Hot Fudge Sauce (see index)

To make shell, beat egg whites and salt until soft peaks form. Gradually add sugar and continue beating until peaks become stiff. Fold in cookies, pecans, vanilla and cream of tartar. Pour into a greased 8-inch pie plate. Bake at 325 degrees for 30-35 minutes. Cool. Smash down crust and place ice cream on top. Freeze. Serve with Hot Fudge Sauce.

6 servings

COFFEE FUDGE PIE

Show ■
Go ■

½ c. slivered almonds
1 T. butter
3 egg whites
1 c. sugar
1 tsp. vanilla
¾ c. chopped walnuts or
  pecans
½ c. finely crushed saltines
1 tsp. baking powder
1 qt. coffee ice cream,
  softened
12 oz. fudge sauce

Sauté almonds in butter until golden. Let cool. Beat egg whites until stiff. Add sugar gradually and add vanilla. Mix nuts, saltines and baking powder; fold into egg whites. Spread on well greased 9-inch pie plate, building up sides. Bake at 300 degrees for 40 minutes until dry on the outside. Cool. Fill with one half of ice cream and spread with fudge sauce. Add remaining ice cream, rest of fudge sauce and sprinkle with almonds. Freeze.

8-10 servings

BUTTER BRICKLE PIE

Show ■
Go ■

2 c. gingersnap crumbs
6 T. butter, melted
½ gal. vanilla ice cream,
  softened
1 (6 oz.) pkg. Bits 'O
  Brickle

Sauce:
½ c. brown sugar
½ c. whipping cream
¼ c. butter
½ c. toasted almonds
1 tsp. vanilla

Combine gingersnap crumbs and butter. Press into greased 9-inch pie plate. Freeze for 30 minutes. Mix ice cream and brickle together. Spread on pie crust. Cover tightly and freeze until ready to use. For sauce, combine sugar, cream and butter in saucepan. Bring to boil, stirring constantly. Remove from heat. Stir in almonds and vanilla. Pass hot sauce with pie.

6-8 servings

May use butter brickle ice cream to make it more "on the go".

BLUEBERRY SOUR CREAM TORTE

Show ■
Go □

Crust:
¾ c. butter, softened
¼ c. sugar
2 egg yolks
2 c. flour
1 tsp. baking powder
½ tsp. salt

Filling:
4 c. fresh blueberries
¾ c. sugar
¼ c. quick cooking tapioca
½ tsp. grated lemon rind
½ tsp. cinnamon
⅛ tsp. nutmeg

Topping:
2 egg yolks, slightly beaten
2 c. dairy sour cream
½ c. sugar
1 tsp. vanilla

For crust, cream butter and sugar. Add egg yolks and beat until fluffy. Combine flour, baking powder and salt and blend into creamed mixture. Press ⅔ of mixture in a 9-inch springform pan. Bake at 400 degrees for 10 minutes. Cool. Reduce oven temperature to 350 degrees. Press remaining crust mixture 1½ inches up side of pan.

For filling, combine berries, sugar, tapioca, lemon rind and spices in saucepan. Let stand 15 minutes. Cook and stir until bubbly and pour into crust.

For topping, blend egg yolks, sour cream, sugar and vanilla. Spoon over fruit filling and bake at 350 degrees for 45 minutes. Let cool and refrigerate until well chilled.

12 servings

Cause for celebration!

FROZEN LEMON TORTE

Show ■
Go ☐

5 lg. eggs, separated
juice of 4 sm. lemons
rind of 1 lemon
2 c. sugar
1 pt. whipping cream
1½ tsp. vanilla
2 (3 oz.) pkgs. ladyfingers
dash of sugar

Beat all 5 egg yolks with 2 egg whites. On low fire, cook the egg mixture, lemon juice, rind and sugar in a double boiler until very thick. Cool thoroughly. Whip the cream with vanilla until stiff. Fold into lemon mixture. Line bottom and sides of a 9-inch springform pan with ladyfingers. Pour lemon mixture in pan and freeze overnight. Before serving, beat 3 egg whites and a dash of sugar until stiff. Pile on frozen torte and place under broiler until lightly browned. Watch carefully. Serve immediately or refreeze.

10-12 servings

LINZERTORTE

Show ■
Go ☐

1½ c. butter
1 c. powdered sugar
1 egg
1½ c. ground filbert nuts
pinch of salt
½ tsp. cinnamon
2¾ c. flour
2 c. raspberry jam
2 tsp. lemon juice
powdered sugar

Cream butter and sugar until light and fluffy. Add egg. Mix together nuts, salt and cinnamon. Stir flour and nut mixture alternately into creamed mixture. Chill dough. Press dough in a 9-inch springform pan, making a 1-inch rim up the side. Reserve a little dough for lattice strips on top. Mix 1½ cups jam and juice and spread over dough. Cut reserve strips of dough and form lattice over jam. Bake at 375 degrees for 40 minutes. When cool, fill squares formed by lattice with extra jam. Sprinkle with powdered sugar.

12-14 servings

CINNAMON TORTE

Show ■
Go ☐

1½ c. butter
2 c. sugar
2 eggs
2¾ c. flour
2 T. cinnamon
butter
½ c. sugar
1 tsp. cinnamon

Filling:
1½ pt. whipping cream
1 (1 oz.) sq. semi-sweet
  chocolate, grated

Topping:
½ pt. whipping cream
2 T. cocoa
2 T. powdered sugar
1 (1 oz.) sq. semi-sweet
  chocolate, grated

Garnish:
5 maraschino cherries,
  drained and dried
sliced almonds
2 T. shaved chocolate

Cream 1½ cups butter and 2 cups sugar. Add eggs. Mix flour and 2 tablespoons cinnamon together and add to creamed mixture. Cut out 16 (9-inch diameter) waxed paper circles. Grease well with butter. Using floured hands, press ⅓ cup of dough to cover each waxed paper circle. Place 2 circles on a greased cookie sheet and bake at 325 degrees for 7 minutes.

Remove from oven; let set 30 seconds, invert onto cooling rack and peel off waxed paper. Mix ½ c. sugar and 1 teaspoon cinnamon and sprinkle a little on waxed paper side of cookie. Cool on rack. Repeat process with remaining circles. Cookies may be made ahead and frozen with waxed paper between each cookie.

For filling, whip cream. Place one cookie on a flat serving dish. Spread with thin layer of whipped cream (about 3 tablespoons per layer). Sprinkle with small amount of grated chocolate. Continue layering with remaining cookies, whipped cream and chocolate. Top with a plain cookie.

For topping, whip cream. Fold in cocoa, powdered sugar and grated chocolate. Spread on top of plain cookie. Do not frost sides. Refrigerate overnight. Before serving, garnish with cherries, almonds and shaved chocolate.

16-18 servings

RHUBARB TORTE

Show ■
Go ☐

Crust:
1 c. Crisco
2 c. flour
2 T. sugar
Filling:
6 egg yolks
2 c. sugar
1 c. half and half cream
¼ c. flour
5 c. diced rhubarb
2 tsp. grated orange rind
Meringue:
6 egg whites
6 T. sugar
¼ tsp. cream of tartar
1 tsp. vanilla
pinch of salt

For crust, mix Crisco, flour and sugar by hand or in food processor. Mixture should be crumbly like a pie crust. Pat into ungreased 9x13-inch pan. Bake at 350 degrees for 10 minutes. For filling, mix together egg yolks, sugar, cream, flour, rhubarb and orange rind. Pour over crust and bake at 350 degrees for 45-50 minutes or until set.

For meringue, beat egg whites until they form a soft peak. Add sugar, cream of tartar, vanilla and salt; spread over filling. Bake at 400 degrees for 2-3 minutes until meringue is golden brown. Cool.

12-14 servings

CHOCOLATE MINT TORTE

Show ■
Go ■

Crust:
1 c. chocolate wafer
    crumbs
2 T. butter, melted
Filling:
½ c. butter, softened
¾ c. sugar
3 (1 oz.) sq. unsweetened
    chocolate, melted
1 tsp. vanilla
¾ tsp. peppermint extract
3 eggs
½ c. whipping cream,
    whipped
shaved chocolate

Combine wafer crumbs and butter. Pat mixture on bottom only of a 9-inch springform pan. Bake at 350 degrees for 7 minutes. Cool. For filling, beat butter until creamy. Gradually add sugar and continue beating until light and fluffy. Mix in chocolate, vanilla and peppermint. Add eggs, one at a time, beating 3 minutes after each addition. Fold in whipped cream. Spoon mixture on crust and sprinkle with shaved chocolate. Freezes well.

10-12 servings

CARAMEL NUT TORTE

Show ■
Go ☐

Crust:
3⅓ c. flour
¼ c. sugar
pinch of salt
1 c. plus 2 T. butter, cut in pieces
2 egg yolks, beaten with 6 T. cold water

Filling:
1½ c. sugar
pinch of cream of tartar
½ c. water
3½ c. chopped pecans or walnuts
½ c. butter
1 c. whipping cream
⅓ c. honey

Icing:
6 oz. semi-sweet chocolate
¼ c. butter
pinch of salt
¾ T. oil

16 pecan or walnut halves

Rich and gooey!

For crust combine flour, sugar and salt in mixer bowl. Beat in butter and egg yolks. Shape into a ball and wrap in waxed paper. Refrigerate 30 minutes only. Roll ⅔ of dough into a 13-inch floured circle. Drape over rolling pin and fit into an ungreased 11-inch flan pan. Leave ¼-inch overhang.

For filling, in a large heavy saucepan, combine sugar, cream of tartar and water. Bring to a boil. Cover and continue boiling over medium heat 1-2 minutes. Uncover and boil until mixture is a light caramel color. This will take about 8 minutes. Remove from heat. Add nuts, butter and whipping cream. Cook over medium heat 5 minutes, reduce to simmer and cook 15 minutes. Stir in honey. Cool slightly. Pour into prepared flan pan.

Roll out remaining dough into an 11-inch circle. Drape over rolling pin and place circle on top of filling. Brush the overhanging bottom dough with water and press over top dough. Cut a 1-inch slit in center of dough and bake at 425 degrees for 20 minutes or until golden brown. Cool at least 4 hours and remove from pan.

For icing, melt chocolate. Add butter, salt and oil; mix well. Spread over top and sides of torte. Decorate with pecan or walnut halves.

16 servings

May be frozen before frosting - but bring to room temperature before spreading icing.

APRICOT CHOCOLATE TORTE

Show ■
Go □

Crust:
3 (1 oz.) sq. unsweetened
  chocolate
2 c. whole walnuts
1½ c. flour
¾ c. light brown sugar,
  firmly packed
½ tsp. salt
½ c. cold butter, cut into
  pieces
2 tsp. cold water
2 tsp. vanilla

Filling:
1 (11 oz.) pkg. dried
  apricots, finely chopped
1½ c. sugar
¾ c. water
3 T. flour
juice of ½ lemon

chocolate shavings

To make crust, place chocolate and nuts in food processor and chop coarsely. Add flour, sugar and salt; blend. (Bits of chocolate and nuts should be visible.) Add butter and process to blend. Add water and vanilla and mix until crumbly. Pat ⅔ of dough onto bottom and 1 inch up the sides in an 8 or 9-inch ungreased springform pan.

Prepare filling in a heavy saucepan by combining all ingredients except chocolate shavings. Bring to boil slowly over low heat. Reduce heat and simmer about 25 minutes, stirring frequently and mashing any large pieces of apricot until mixture resembles thick jam. Remove from heat and cool. Place filling in crust and crumble additional dough over top to cover. Bake at 350 degrees for 40 minutes and cool.

To serve, remove springform and decorate top with chocolate shavings.

10-12 servings

TIA MARIA TORTE

Show ■
Go ■

2 lbs. crisp chocolate chip
  cookies
1 c. milk
6 oz. Tia Maria liqueur
1 pt. whipping cream
3 T. powdered sugar
1 tsp. vanilla
shaved chocolate
sliced almonds

Dip cookies in milk and then in liqueur. Arrange some cookies on bottom and sides of 8-inch springform pan. Whip cream with sugar and vanilla. Alternate whipped cream with layer of dipped cookies, ending with whipped cream. Top with chocolate and almonds. Refrigerate.

12-15 servings

STRAWBERRY PIZZA

Show ■
Go □

Crust:
1 c. flour
¼ c. powdered sugar
½ c. frozen unsalted butter

Filling:
1 (8 oz.) pkg. cream cheese, softened
½ c. sugar
1 tsp. vanilla
½ tsp. almond extract
1 qt. fresh strawberries, washed, hulled and dried

Glaze:
1 (6 oz.) jar red currant jelly
1½ T. lemon juice

whipped cream

For crust, cut flour, powdered sugar and butter together. Pat evenly over a 12 or 13-inch greased pizza pan. Press firmly and bake at 325 degrees for 15-20 minutes until lightly browned. Cool.

For filling, combine cream cheese, sugar, vanilla and almond extract and spread over cooled crust. On filling, arrange strawberries in circles starting at outside edge and ending with a large strawberry in the center.

Make glaze by heating jelly over low heat until melted. Add lemon juice. Drizzle glaze over fruit. Top with whipped cream.

10 servings

May use fresh fruits such as kiwi, grapes, raspberries, pineapple.

CHOCOLATE "HIPPO"

Show ■
Go ■

1 pt. whipping cream
1 (16 oz.) can Hershey's chocolate syrup
1-3 T. Grand Marnier, Creme de Cacao or Kirsch liqueur
chocolate shavings

Whip cream until it is very stiff. Fold in chocolate syrup and liqueur thoroughly. Place in miniature soufflé cups and freeze. Serve frozen. Sprinkle chocolate shavings on top of each soufflé.

14 servings

ECLAIR SQUARES

Show ■
Go ■

12 oz. (approximately 21) graham crackers

Filling:
2 (3¾ oz.) pkgs. French vanilla instant pudding
3 c. milk
1 (8 oz.) carton Cool Whip, thawed

Frosting:
2 (1 oz.) sq. unsweetened chocolate
2 T. light corn syrup
3 T. butter or margarine
1½ c. powdered sugar
3 T. milk
½ tsp. vanilla

Prepare one to two days before serving. Lightly butter a 9x13-inch pan. Spread one layer of graham crackers on bottom of pan. Beat pudding and milk in a large bowl. Blend in Cool Whip. Cover with half of pudding mixture. Repeat layer process again, ending with graham crackers.

For frosting, melt chocolate and add remaining ingredients. Blend well and spread on top of graham crackers. Refrigerate for one to two days before serving.

16 pieces

BANANAS FOSTER BLUE HORSE

Show ■
Go ■

1 c. butter
1 c. brown sugar
1 oz. Creme de Banana liqueur
4 med. bananas
1 oz. white rum
4 scoops vanilla ice cream

In a crêpe pan or 10-inch skillet, melt butter and brown sugar. Add Creme de Banana and blend thoroughly. Cut peeled bananas in half lengthwise and once crosswise and place flat side down into mixture. Sauté on both sides until tender. Now for show, heat rum in small pan, pour over bananas and light with match. Spoon banana mixture over ice cream in serving dishes.

4 servings

Other Good Stuff

STEAK MARINADE

Show ■
Go □

1 T. red wine vinegar
2 T. ketchup
3 T. oil
3 T. soy sauce
¼ tsp. pepper
1 clove garlic, crushed

Mix all ingredients and pour over meat. Marinate at least 3 hours or overnight.

½ cup

PESTO SAUCE

Show ■
Go ■

2 c. fresh basil leaves
½ c. olive oil
2 T. pignoli (pine nuts)
2 cloves garlic, crushed
1 tsp. salt
½ c. freshly grated
Parmesan cheese
2 T. freshly grated Romano
cheese
3 T. butter, softened

In blender or food processor mix together the basil, oil, pine nuts, garlic, salt and cheeses; then add the butter.

2¾ cups

MAYONNAISE

Show ■
Go ■

1 egg
1 tsp. fresh lemon juice
1 tsp. red wine vinegar
1-2 tsp. Dijon mustard
1 tsp. salt
freshly ground white
pepper
1¼ c. safflower oil
¼ c. olive oil

In food processor or blender, mix egg, lemon juice, vinegar, mustard, salt and pepper. Combine oils. Add 3 tablespoons to egg mixture. Process for 5 seconds. With motor running, add remaining oil in a steady stream until mayonnaise thickens. When thick add remaining oil quickly.

1½ cups

MUSHROOM SAUCE

Show ■
Go ■

4½ T. butter
8 oz. fresh mushrooms,
    sliced
3 T. flour
¾ c. milk
¾ c. whipping cream
salt to taste
pepper to taste
⅛ tsp. nutmeg
1 c. shredded Swiss cheese
1 egg yolk
¼ c. dry white wine

In small skillet, melt 2 tablespoons butter and sauté mushrooms 4 minutes. Set aside. In medium saucepan, melt remaining 2½ tablespoons butter. Blend in flour and gradually stir in milk and cream. Bring to a boil. Season with salt, pepper and nutmeg. Stir in cheese until melted. Beat egg yolk with wine and add to mixture. Cook 1 minute, add mushrooms and reheat a few minutes.

3½ cups

FRESH HERB BUTTER

Show ■
Go ■

½ c. finely chopped fresh
    parsley
½ c. finely chopped fresh
    dill
2 marjoram leaves,
    chopped
4 green onions, finely
    chopped
1 tsp. lemon balm or
    verbena (optional)
1 lb. butter, margarine or
    cream cheese, softened
¼ tsp. salt
¼ tsp. pepper
¼ tsp. crushed garlic

Blend herbs and butter. Add salt, pepper and garlic. Place in crock and store in refrigerator. Serve on homemade bread, potatoes, vegetables, steak or chicken.

1 pound

Fresh herbs are a must.

SWEET DILL MUSTARD

Show ■
Go ■

1 c. dry mustard
1 c. cider vinegar
¾ c. sugar
¼ c. water
2 tsp. salt
1½ tsp. dill weed
2 eggs, slightly beaten

In small bowl, combine mustard, vinegar, sugar, water, salt and dill weed. Let stand at room temperature 4-6 hours. Stir in eggs. Cook mixture in double boiler about 8-10 minutes, stirring occasionally. Cool, cover and refrigerate at least 24 hours before using. If mustard is too thick, thin with white wine.

2 cups

SHALLOT BUTTER

Show ■
Go ■

4½ oz. shallots
4½ oz. butter, softened

In hot water, blanch shallots, quickly drain and squeeze well in cloth. Chop until fine. Add butter and mix. For a finer texture, press through sieve.

¼ cup

PICKLES FOREVER

Show ■
Go □

8 thinly sliced cucumbers
  (peeled or unpeeled)
1½ c. thinly sliced onions
1½ T. salt
1 c. sliced celery
1 green pepper, sliced
2 c. sugar
1 c. white vinegar
1½ tsp. mustard seed
1 tsp. celery seed

Combine cucumbers, onions, salt, celery and green pepper; let stand 30 minutes. Drain off liquid. Mix sugar, vinegar, mustard seed and celery seed together; add to cucumber mixture. Refrigerate. More vegetables may be added as needed.

10 cups

SPICED GREEN PEPPER JELLY

Show ■
Go ■

**3 lg. green peppers,
seeded and finely
chopped**
½ c. white vinegar
6½ c. sugar
**3 T. crushed dry red
pepper**
2 (3 oz.) pkgs. Certo
**5 drops green food
coloring**

In a medium saucepan, combine peppers, vinegar, sugar and red pepper; bring to a rolling boil. Add Certo and return to a boil. Skim green foam and continue boiling for 2 minutes. Add coloring and skim again. Pour in small jars; cover and refrigerate. Serve spread on block of cream cheese, with snack bread or crackers.

3 pints

THE PLANNER'S GINGERY PLUM CHUTNEY

Show ■
Go □

1 c. sugar
**1 c. light brown sugar,
firmly packed**
¾ c. cider vinegar
**1½ tsp. crushed red
pepper**
2 tsp. salt
2 tsp. mustard seed
3 cloves garlic, crushed
¼ c. grated onion
**½ c. thinly sliced
preserved ginger and
juice**
1 c. golden raisins
**1 qt. fresh Italian prune
plums**

Cook all ingredients except plums in Dutch oven (or crockpot turned to 300 degrees) over high heat, stirring occasionally until sugar is dissolved. Halve and pit plums and add to Dutch oven. Cover. Turn heat to low (crockpot to 200 degrees) and cook 2-3 hours. (It will take 4-6 hours in a crockpot but needs very little watching.) Stir occasionally. Can remove cover and cook down to desired consistency. Ladle into hot sterilized jars and seal. (If kept in refrigerator canning jars are not necessary.)

3 pints

Wonderful hostess gifts!

CARAMEL NUT SAUCE

Show ■
Go ■

½ c. brown sugar, packed
½ c. light corn syrup
2 T. butter
⅛ tsp. salt
¾ c. chopped toasted
   pecans
¼ c. whipping cream
1 tsp. vanilla

Combine sugar, syrup, butter and salt in medium saucepan. Stir over medium heat until sugar is dissolved. Remove from heat. Stir in nuts, cream and vanilla. Serve hot over ice cream.

2 cups

CARAMEL SAUCE

Show ■
Go □

1¼ c. sugar
½ c. butter
1 c. whipping cream

In heavy skillet, over very low heat, cook sugar until brown. Watch carefully to avoid burning. Do not stir, but frequently shake pan. It will take 30-40 minutes for sugar to turn to a brown liquid. Stir in butter. When butter is melted, it will be separated on top of sugar. Over low heat, with wooden spoon, blend in cream, stirring constantly until mixture is smooth. Sauce may be stored in covered container in refrigerator up to 1 week. Before serving, heat sauce in top of double boiler. Serve as a topping for ice cream.

2 cups

HOT FUDGE SAUCE

Show ■
Go ■

1 c. sugar
3 T. flour
¼ tsp. salt
1¼ c. milk
2 (1 oz.) sq. unsweetened
   chocolate (or 2 packets
   of pre-melted chocolate)

Combine dry ingredients in saucepan; add milk and chocolate. Cook over medium heat, stirring frequently until chocolate melts and ingredients come to a boil. Sauce will thicken as it cooks. Remove from heat and serve.

If sauce is too thick, slowly add a little warm milk, stirring until proper consistency is reached. Also can be reheated, uncovered, in the microwave for 1-2 minutes depending on the amount left. A few drops of peppermint flavoring may be added.

1½ cups

HOT FUDGE/CARAMEL SAUCE

Show ■
Go ■

½ c. whole milk
1 lb. caramels
½ lb. semi-sweet chocolate
½ pt. vanilla ice cream,
   softened
1 tsp. vanilla

Heat milk and caramels in double boiler until caramels are melted. Chop chocolate and add to caramel mixture. Add ice cream and vanilla. Blend; heat and serve.

3 cups

Just a spoonful of fudge sauce makes the medicine go down.

M&M CARAMEL CORN

Show ■
Go ■

½ c. light corn syrup
1⅓ c. sugar
1 c. butter
2 qts. popped popcorn
2 c. mixed nuts
1-1½ c. M&M candies

Combine syrup, sugar and butter in medium saucepan and bring to boil. Continue boiling on low heat to hard ball stage. Combine popcorn, nuts and M&M's in a large bowl. Pour syrup over top and mix together. Spread on a greased jelly roll pan. Refrigerate until cold. Break into pieces.

3 quarts

CARAMEL PUFF-CORN

Show ■
Go ■

2 (5 oz.) bags puffcorn curls or hulless popped corn
1 lb. nuts (optional)
1½ c. butter
3 c. brown sugar, firmly packed
¾ c. light or dark corn syrup
½ tsp. baking soda
1 tsp. vanilla

Place puffcorn curls and nuts in large roasting pan. Combine butter, brown sugar and corn syrup in a heavy 4-quart saucepan. Cook over medium heat, stirring until sugar is dissolved and all ingredients are mixed. Bring to a boil and boil for 5 minutes. Remove from heat; stir in baking soda and vanilla. Pour hot syrup over puffcorn, stirring to mix and coat well. Bake uncovered at 250 degrees for 1 hour, stirring every 15 minutes. Let cool and continue to stir so it doesn't stick to pan. Store in airtight containers.

5 quarts

PEANUT CLUSTERS

Show ■
Go ■

1 lb. white almond bark
1 (12 oz.) pkg. chocolate chips
1 lb. Spanish peanuts

Melt bark and chocolate chips in double boiler or microwave. Mix in peanuts. Drop by teaspoonfuls onto waxed paper. Cool. Remove and serve plain or place in paper candy cups.

3 dozen

NUT GOODIE BAR CANDY

Show ■
Go □

1 (12 oz.) pkg. chocolate chips
1 (12 oz.) pkg. butterscotch chips
2 c. creamy peanut butter
1 (1 oz.) sq. unsweetened chocolate
1 c. butter
⅓ c. evaporated or ½ c. regular milk
¼ c. regular vanilla pudding mix
2 lbs. powdered sugar
1 tsp. maple flavoring
½ lb. Spanish peanuts, skinned

In double boiler or microwave, melt chips, peanut butter and chocolate. Spread half of the melted chocolate mixture in a foil-lined buttered, 10½x15½-inch jelly roll pan. Refrigerate or freeze until set (about 30 minutes in freezer). Reserve remaining chocolate mixture in double boiler.

In heavy saucepan, combine butter, milk and pudding mix. Bring to boil over low heat and cook 1 minute. Remove and let cool. Using a mixer, blend in powdered sugar and flavoring until creamy. Spread mixture over chilled chocolate. Stir Spanish peanuts into remaining chocolate mixture and spread over top. Refrigerate for 3 hours. Peel off foil and cut into 1-inch squares. Keep refrigerated.

150 pieces

GRANOLA CANDY

Show ■
Go ■

1 (12 oz.) pkg. chocolate chips
1 (12 oz.) pkg. butterscotch chips
1½ c. salted mixed nuts
1½ c. 100% natural cereal with raisins and dates

In double boiler, melt chocolate and butterscotch chips. Add nuts and cereal; mix well. Line a 10½x15½-inch jelly roll pan with greased waxed paper. Spread candy mixture evenly in pan and refrigerate. When set, cut or break into pieces.

20-25 pieces

ENGLISH TOFFEE

Show ■
Go □

2 c. butter
2½ c. sugar
1½ c. whole unblanched
   almonds
3 c. chocolate chips
1½ c. chopped walnuts

In heavy skillet, melt butter. Add sugar and cook over moderate heat, stirring often, until mixture foams vigorously. Turn heat to low; cook and stir 5 minutes longer. Add almonds and cook over medium heat until nuts begin to pop, about 10 minutes. Lower heat and cook 7 minutes, stirring occasionally. Pour into a 10½x15½-inch jelly roll pan and cool until it hardens. Melt chocolate chips and spread ½ over top of cooled candy. Sprinkle ¾ cup walnuts on top of chocolate. Cool. Flip onto board. Spread other side with remaining chocolate and walnuts. Cool and break into pieces.

40 pieces

What a way to "waist" calories!

CARAMEL NUT CANDY

Show ■
Go ☐

**2 (12 oz.) pkgs. chocolate
 chips**
**2 lbs. assorted nuts or
 salted peanuts**
3 c. brown sugar
1 c. butter
1 c. light corn syrup
**1 (14 oz.) can sweetened
 condensed milk**

Line sides and bottom of a 10½x15½-inch jelly roll pan with foil; butter foil. In double boiler, melt chocolate chips over low heat and spread half of it in thin layer on the foil. Sprinkle nuts over hot chocolate. Mix together sugar, butter, syrup and milk and cook very slowly until it reaches soft ball stage or 240 degrees on a candy thermometer. Spread on top of nuts. Let cool 5 minutes. Spread remaining chocolate on top of caramel layer. Refrigerate until set. Lift out of pan and remove foil. Cut into 1-inch squares and place in paper candy cups.

150 pieces

Things to Know

ABBREVIATIONS

tsp. = teaspoon	pt. = pint	lg. = large	gal. = gallon
T. = tablespoon	qt. = quart	med. = medium	sq. = square
c. = cup	oz. = ounce	lb. = pound	pkg. = package

WEIGHTS AND MEASURES

3 tsp. = 1 T.	5⅓ T. = ⅓ c.	1 lb. = 16 oz.	4 c. = 1 qt.
2 T. = 1 fluid oz.	8 T. = ½ c.	1 c. = ½ pt.	4 qt. = 1 gal.
4 T. = 1/4 c.	16 T. = 1 c.	2 c. = 1 pt.	

SUBSTITUTIONS AND EQUIVALENTS

2 T. butter = 1 oz.
4 T. butter = ¼ c.
1 c. butter = ½ lb.
2 c. butter = 1 lb.
2 c. sugar = 1 lb.
2 ¼ c. packed brown sugar = 1 lb.
1 ⅓ c. packed brown sugar = 1 c. granulated sugar
3 ½ c. powdered sugar = 1 lb.
4 c. sifted all purpose flour = 1 lb.
4 ½ c. sifted cake flour = 1 lb.
1 oz. chocolate = 1 sq.
3 T. cocoa & 1 T. fat = 1 oz. chocolate
1 c. egg whites = 8-10 whites

1 c. egg yolks = 12-14 yolks
25 marshmallows = ¼ lb.
1 T. cornstarch = 2 T. flour for thickening
1 T. vinegar or lemon juice & 1 c. milk = 1 c. sour milk
10 graham crackers = 1 c. fine crumbs
1 c. whipping cream = 2 c. whipped
1 lemon = 3-4 T. juice
1 orange = 6-8 T. juice
1 c. uncooked rice = 3-4 c. cooked rice.

Index

FOOD FOR SHOW! *food on the go!*

Mount Sinai Auxiliary
2215 Park Ave., Minneapolis, MN 55404
612-871-3700   Ext. 1828

Please send me _____ copies
Food For Show/Food On The Go at **$9.95** ea. _____
Add postage & handling at **$1.25** ea. _____
[NOTE: Postage is $.50 per book on orders]
[of 6 or more books mailed to one address.]

Minnesota residents add 6% sales tax at **$ .60** ea. _____

TOTAL $ _____

NAME

ADDRESS

CITY   STATE   ZIP

Please make checks payable to: COOKBOOK, Mount Sinai Auxiliary.
All proceeds from sale of cookbook will benefit Mount Sinai Auxiliary's commitment to the
Development Fund. For gifts, please include cards and a list of addresses.

FOOD FOR SHOW! *food on the go!*

Mount Sinai Auxiliary
2215 Park Ave., Minneapolis, MN 55404
612-871-3700   Ext. 1828

Please send me _____ copies
Food For Show/Food On The Go at **$9.95** ea. _____
Add postage & handling at **$1.25** ea. _____
[NOTE: Postage is $.50 per book on orders]
[of 6 or more books mailed to one address.]

Minnesota residents add 6% sales tax at **$ .60** ea. _____

TOTAL $ _____

NAME

ADDRESS

CITY   STATE   ZIP

Please make checks payable to: COOKBOOK, Mount Sinai Auxiliary.
All proceeds from sale of cookbook will benefit Mount Sinai Auxiliary's commitment to the
Development Fund. For gifts, please include cards and a list of addresses.

FOOD FOR SHOW! *food on the go!*

Mount Sinai Auxiliary
2215 Park Ave., Minneapolis, MN 55404
612-871-3700   Ext. 1828

Please send me _____ copies
Food For Show/Food On The Go at **$9.95** ea. _____
Add postage & handling at **$1.25** ea. _____
[NOTE: Postage is $.50 per book on orders]
[of 6 or more books mailed to one address.]

Minnesota residents add 6% sales tax at **$ .60** ea. _____

TOTAL $ _____

NAME

ADDRESS

CITY   STATE   ZIP

Please make checks payable to: COOKBOOK, Mount Sinai Auxiliary.
All proceeds from sale of cookbook will benefit Mount Sinai Auxiliary's commitment to the
Development Fund. For gifts, please include cards and a list of addresses.

FOOD
FOR
SHOW!
food on the go!

Mount Sinai Auxiliary
2215 Park Ave., Minneapolis, MN 55404
612-871-3700   Ext. 1828

Please send me _____ copies
Food For Show/Food On The Go at **$9.95** ea. _____
Add postage & handling at **$1.25** ea. _____
[NOTE: Postage is $.50 per book on orders
of 6 or more books mailed to one address.]

Minnesota residents add 6% sales tax at **$ .60** ea. _____

TOTAL $ _____

NAME

ADDRESS

CITY   STATE   ZIP

Please make checks payable to: COOKBOOK, Mount Sinai Auxiliary.
All proceeds from sale of cookbook will benefit Mount Sinai Auxiliary's commitment to the
Development Fund. For gifts, please include cards and a list of addresses.

- -

FOOD
FOR
SHOW!
food on the go!

Mount Sinai Auxiliary
2215 Park Ave., Minneapolis, MN 55404
612-871-3700   Ext. 1828

Please send me _____ copies
Food For Show/Food On The Go at **$9.95** ea. _____
Add postage & handling at **$1.25** ea. _____
[NOTE: Postage is $.50 per book on orders
of 6 or more books mailed to one address.]

Minnesota residents add 6% sales tax at **$ .60** ea. _____

TOTAL $ _____

NAME

ADDRESS

CITY   STATE   ZIP

Please make checks payable to: COOKBOOK, Mount Sinai Auxiliary.
All proceeds from sale of cookbook will benefit Mount Sinai Auxiliary's commitment to the
Development Fund. For gifts, please include cards and a list of addresses.

- -

FOOD
FOR
SHOW!
food on the go!

Mount Sinai Auxiliary
2215 Park Ave., Minneapolis, MN 55404
612-871-3700   Ext. 1828

Please send me _____ copies
Food For Show/Food On The Go at **$9.95** ea. _____
Add postage & handling at **$1.25** ea. _____
[NOTE: Postage is $.50 per book on orders
of 6 or more books mailed to one address.]

Minnesota residents add 6% sales tax at **$ .60** ea. _____

TOTAL $ _____

NAME

ADDRESS

CITY   STATE   ZIP

Please make checks payable to: COOKBOOK, Mount Sinai Auxiliary.
All proceeds from sale of cookbook will benefit Mount Sinai Auxiliary's commitment to the
Development Fund. For gifts, please include cards and a list of addresses.